"If you've ever wished your most be come to life and guide you throug you're in luck. In *Mothering by the* ___ pito pairs her own hard-earned insights with truth, advice, and transformative life tools from the classic characters we know and love. The result? Wit and wisdom for every mother, everywhere."

—Erin Loechner, author of *Chasing Slow*

"Jennifer Pepito is a mother of unparalleled principle and passion. With vulnerable reflection and seasoned wisdom, she shows us how literature can not only entertain and educate, but also help us reframe our values, revive our confidence, and recapture the magic of motherhood."

—Ainsley Arment, author of *The Call of the Wild + Free*

"In *Mothering by the Book*, Jennifer Pepito declares that literature can shape your worldview, dispel narcissism, and allow you to walk in another person's shoes, if only for a few brief pages. Her words will call you to courageous parenting by pointing you back to the books of your childhood."

—Jamie Erickson, author of *Homeschool Bravely: How to Squash Doubt, Trust God, and Teach Your Child with Confidence* and *Holy Hygge: Creating a Place for People to Gather and the Gospel to Grow*

"*Mothering by the Book* is a beautiful collection of wise insight and gentle guidance from a mentor. Jennifer generously offers stories from her life alongside classic literature and Scripture to speak right to a mother's heart. *Mothering by the Book* is inspiring, engaging, and practical; it reminds us that we're not alone, and that there is always hope."

—Leah Boden, author of *Moments on Mothering*

"In *Mothering by the Book*, Jennifer Pepito rejects the common veil of perfect motherhood to reveal a beautifully messy and inspiring journey that my mama heart immediately recognizes as truth. Her words are a balm that leaves me feeling seen and known. By uniquely tying the lessons of life's trials and triumphs to living literature and God's Word, Jennifer Pepito gifts mothers a sincere hope while reminding us of the incomparably fierce power of a mother's love."

—Amber O'Neal Johnston, author of *A Place to Belong*

"I loved reading about Jennifer's experiences as a mother of many. Her deep understanding of our fears and motivations made her story not only familiar but hopeful. *Mothering by the Book* is full of the ups and downs of walking with Christ in the midst of crazy large-family logistics."

—Cindy Rollins, author of *Mere Motherhood*

"This is not just another parenting book; Jennifer has captured something deeper and more profound—how to overcome the pestilent fears that rob us of experiencing joy, peace, and fulfillment. This book will transform you, your marriage, your relationship with your children, and most of all, your relationship with God."

—Jeannie Fulbright, MFA, author of the Young Explorer Series

"Jennifer Pepito shows us how we can rewrite the story of fear in our own lives so we can shepherd our children well. Masterfully weaving together beloved books, Scriptures, and vulnerable truths from her own life, Jennifer helps us create an environment of peace, joy, fun, and presence in our families."

—Christine Marie Bailey, author of *The Kindred Life*

"As a mother who deeply cherishes the formative value of rich literature not only in my children's lives but also in my own heart, I adore this book. Jennifer weaves some of our family's favorite read-alouds along with biblical truth throughout this book to equip readers to choose faith over fear. Her profound insight on motherhood and carefully chosen examples from literature breathed fresh insight, encouragement, and joy into my heart. *Mothering by the Book* is a true treasure for all mamas."

—Dr. Ashley Turner, author of *Restorative Kitchen*

Mothering by the BOOK

Mothering by the BOOK

THE POWER *of* READING ALOUD *to* OVERCOME FEAR *and* RECAPTURE JOY

JENNIFER PEPITO

BETHANYHOUSE

a division of Baker Publishing Group
Minneapolis, Minnesota

Published by Bethany House Publishers
11400 Hampshire Avenue South
Minneapolis, Minnesota 55438
www.bethanyhouse.com

Bethany House Publishers is a division of
Baker Publishing Group, Grand Rapids, Michigan

Printed in the United States of America

Library of Congress Cataloging-in-Publication Data
Names: Pepito, Jennifer, author.
Title: Mothering by the book : the power of reading aloud to overcome fear and
    recapture joy / Jennifer Pepito.
Description: Minneapolis, MN : Bethany House Publishers, a division of Baker
    Publishing Group, 2022.
Identifiers: LCCN 2022002990 | ISBN 9780764239533 (paperback) | ISBN
    9780764240751 (casebound) | ISBN 9781493437405 (ebook)
Subjects: LCSH: Fear. | Joy. | Parenting. | Oral reading. | Reading (Early childhood) |
    Children—Books and reading.
Classification: LCC BF575.F2 P454 2022 | DDC 152.4/6—dc23/eng/20220307
LC record available at https://lccn.loc.gov/2022002990

Cover design by Kelly L. Howard

Jennifer Pepito is represented by Ingrid Beck.

Baker Publishing Group publications use paper produced from sustainable forestry practices and post-consumer waste whenever possible.

22 23 24 25 26 27 28   7 6 5 4 3 2 1

To Emelie, Eden, Elias, Ethan,
Emmett, Ella, and Ezra.
Being your mom is my greatest joy,
and I'm so grateful for all the love and
grace you have shown me
on this journey.

To Scott. I'm so glad we get
to grow old together.

To the younger me and all of you
who see yourself in my story.
Don't be afraid, God is with you.

Contents

Foreword

As a shy introvert, I have been called to a life in the public arena, where I am constantly forced to live outside my comfort zone—speaking to large groups, mingling with many strangers, smiling through hours of sharing myself as women stand in long lines to chat after I am through speaking. I cherish the life I have, but sometimes it is a bit of a stretch for my personality.

Some years ago, I boarded a train to Stratford-on-Avon in England from where I was living in Oxford. I was so very honored to be asked to speak at a Wild + Free home education conference. I rose above my insecurities and made a commitment to be engaged in the experience. The morning the conference began, I sought the building and the room where the speakers were to meet. Heart beating wildly, I convinced myself that I would surely forge friendships with some of these kindred spirits.

As I slowly began to merge into the crowd of women who seemed to already know one another, a gentle, friendly voice called to me, "Sally, come over here. I am so excited that you were able to come join us. I've known of you for a long time and was hoping we would meet someday!"

Jennifer Pepito was the name of this lovely woman who turned the conference around for me—from questionable weekend to one of sweet memories made, with inspiration sprinkled every hour and my feeling that I was "one of the crowd" with women I so admired.

Since that time, I have had many opportunities to get to know Jennifer better. When I am with her, I always come away feeling more ready to take on all that life holds. She encourages, affirms, and takes every opportunity to make those in her life feel they are special. She knows a hidden treasure of story, love, humor, and spiritual strength rests inside many of us that probably will never be known or seen by others, yet it lives within us nonetheless.

Jennifer is a woman rich in so many ways that at first were hidden from me, and yet were revealed delightfully through many encounters as a friend. As I have learned more of her life story, I have come to understand that she has walked faithfully, full-heartedly through many seasons of life. Through the years, she stored up tales of generous love for children and a wholehearted acceptance of the story of her marriage; she moved fearlessly through hardships when life felt out of control or didn't match her expectations, learning that education and inspiration are about storytelling that captures the imagination—and so much more. All of these treasures and many others are contained and revealed in *Mothering by the Book*.

Jennifer companions us, and through her words, her honesty about her struggles, and her joy in the moments, she makes us feel seen, understood. Her focus on epic books and stories calls us to live with freedom, grace for ourselves, and appreciation for each adventure and challenge along the way. I know this book will become beloved and will be read many times by those who find it.

Thank you, Jennifer, for giving us hope and a sense of confidence to risk living our own lives with delight, freedom, and celebration.

—Sally Clarkson, author of *Awaking Wonder*, *Help, I'm Drowning*, and *The Lifegiving Home*, Oxford, 2022

Let Literature Free Us from Fear

There are no "if's" in God's world. And no places that are safer
than other places. The center of His will is our only safety.

Betsie ten Boom quoted in Corrie ten Boom, *The Hiding Place*

As we drove down the road with the late-afternoon sun
streaming into our truck, I hung up the phone, kicked
my feet against the dash, and cried, "I can't take this
anymore," before bursting into tears. My five children were
squeezed into the back seat, frozen in shock and wide-eyed
at my outburst. The emotional meltdown had been precipi-
tated by yet another hard no in my search for a place for
our family to stay—somewhere to escape from the crowded
campgrounds we'd called home for the last few months.

We were living small in a thirty-foot travel trailer. And
while I didn't mind the tiny home, I hated having neighbors
so close. RVs with thin walls were lined up tightly like horses

in rodeo chutes, and this life was starting to get old. It was winter in Southern California, and my overactive imagination was causing me anxiety as I worried about offending the elderly "snowbirds" looking for a quiet spot to camp for the winter who might instead end up next to a loud family of seven. It was a beautiful place for nature study, with exotic moths flying among the fragrant eucalyptus trees, but I was desperate to find a less conspicuous place to park our home while we worked on building a mission base just across the border in Mexico. I was getting us through each day by quietly homeschooling in the trailer and following up with an hour of PBS Kids after lunch, until I felt we'd spent enough time on schoolwork to deflect awkward questions with proof of our scholarly diligence. Then, when I felt the coast was clear, I would let the kids out to play without worrying that I'd be reported for educational neglect by curious and closed-minded neighbors.

It wasn't easy keeping three little boys—as well as a daughter with sensory processing disorder—calm and quiet in these conditions, but with the help of my stalwart oldest daughter, we were managing. We worked hard to keep the tiny space tidy in order to help my younger daughter feel comfortable and to avoid conflicts. I didn't want our family to be noisy neighbors and attract unwanted attention, and I was desperate for a change, hopeful that a nearby Christian camp would let us rent a space so my kids could play freely outside instead of being scrutinized by retirees who were critical of homeschooling. The stress of keeping my family cared for in the fishbowl of the campground was wearing on me, and I was careening toward a breaking point.

It didn't help matters at all that my husband and I were quietly raging at each other, each blaming the other for the discomfort of the present circumstances. The missionary adventure had worn us out, and we could barely speak without erupting into a fight—a far cry from our formerly tranquil relationship. Many years after this trailer-life experience, I watched a short clip of a parody on modern culture, *Portlandia*. In this short video, the characters romanticize van life and then endure its uncomfortable reality. The clip ends with the wife giving her husband the bird as she hitchhikes her way out of there. I giggled nervously at how closely it reflected our own experience. That is, I never gave my husband the middle finger, nor did I run off with a stranger, but I probably imagined doing both during the depths of this hard season. The tight quarters with zero personal space and trying to keep children happy and quiet with close neighbors were irritating enough, but with our added marital difficulties, the situation felt unbearable.

But what was really so awful about my life that I would fall apart in front of my children, kicking the dash like a two-year-old just because the Christian camp said no to our parking the trailer there? What was so bad that I would shriek like a cat in disappointment, causing my children stress and anxiety, when all I wanted was to give them a happy childhood? Why couldn't I find the joy in the life we were living, instead of constantly comparing the present circumstances with what I now idealized as the children's paradise I had created before we left our home to become missionaries? Why was I so full of fear and despair?

The truth is, there was nothing so awful about my life. But there was a lot wrong inside my head. Fear was rendering me incapacitated. I worried about the future of our family because my husband and I couldn't talk to each other without descending into a quarrel. I worried about my children having a crappy childhood, all the while wrecking it with my anxiety and unthankfulness. I was afraid of failing as a mother, of living in Mexico, of my children getting sick or hurt. The list of fears seemed to be endless, and the joy and wonder of motherhood was being decimated as a wily enemy kept me dead to the true beauty of my life.

Fear Was Pushing Me Around

I was intent on loving my children well, but the myths I believed about my capability, my circumstances, and even God's faithfulness caused inner anguish as I let the giants of fear and worry push me around. All this time spent contemplating the what-ifs kept me from enjoying my children. In her book *Breaking the Fear Cycle*, Maria Furlough writes, "So often our fears take us inward. They suck us into the details of our lives, our homes, our jobs, and our futures, and we forget that God's plan is so much bigger than the minute details of our lives."[1] This was happening to me. I was being sucked inward and missing the beautiful big picture of what we were experiencing as a family. I was missing the growth and the character that was being developed because my vision was so narrow. And I was missing the joy. Instead of running through the woods with my children, I was inside feeling depressed and afraid. Instead of being thankful for the freedom and simplicity of that season in the trailer, I grumbled at the circumstances, afraid we were ruining our children by depriving them of my vision of a perfect childhood.

As I remained stuck, worrying about the future, these fears robbed me of many magical moments and nearly robbed me of my life. But I was a Charlotte Mason method homeschool mom, so even though I was caught up in a swirl of fears that led me into depression, I was diligently reading aloud to my children. I'd sit with these children's classics, my own babies tucked in close, and as I read, these books saved my life. I read through *The Long Winter* while enduring my own long winter as a missionary in Mexico, and I was empowered to believe that my family would make it through. I read *Pride and Prejudice* while at war with my husband and was encouraged that if Lizzy and Mr. Darcy could overcome their difficulties, we could too. I read *Endurance*, a story about a feat of survival in Antarctica, and knew I could survive and thrive in my own survival story as a mom of many. I recaptured the magic of motherhood by fighting fear with stories and letting the truth of Scripture hammer it home.

> I recaptured the magic of motherhood by fighting fear with stories and letting the truth of Scripture hammer it home.

Childhood Is Too Precious to Waste

Through this book, I want to help you recapture the magic of motherhood as well. Childhood is too precious to waste, and our children need us to be present so they can be empowered to kill their own giants. Fear keeps us in our heads, imagining the worst about ourselves and our circumstances, and fear is a slippery little demon that masquerades well. You might be bold as a lion when it comes to confrontation but cower in the face of sickness. You might be as calm as Clara Barton when dealing with a medical emergency but crippled with anxiety in social situations. Maybe you are in your element in a crowd but feel like a deer in the headlights when juggling the needs of infants and toddlers—full of fears about future failure because of present inadequacy. One friend of mine is a bold performer, singing in front of hundreds of people, but the thought of having a fifth child caused her to stumble in fear. Another friend was afraid that homeschooling would cause strife between her and her children. Still another finds that worry about mothering through the high school years consumes her. Fear looms large in our mothering journey. It comes in so many different packages, but when we fixate on fear, we become blind to the beauty around us. Elizabeth Barrett Browning said, "Earth's crammed with heaven, / And every common bush afire with God; / But only he who sees, takes off his shoes."[2]

Here is what we will do to recapture motherhood's magic: Instead of being blinded to the beauty of our own present life by the fears we believe about the future, we will learn to see. We will open our senses to the twinkle in our child's eyes, the smell of fresh laundry on the line, the feel of a baby's warm body pressed close to ours as they take their nourishment. We won't squander this season with worry; we'll wring every bit of joy out of each moment. We will learn how to take our thoughts captive and reject the lies that keep us afraid and incapacitated. We will learn how to be present and experience the presence of God. We will learn how to be free.

When we identify the fears that steal the magic from our lives, and even identify the trauma that originated those fears, we can tear them down. We can take up our trusty motherhood tools, our literature and our liturgy, the Word and the wonder, and be ready and able to savor this fleeting journey of motherhood. We will join the cloud of witnesses who have overcome fear themselves—Corrie, Ma, Harriet, and Shackleton—and let them lead us into freedom.

In *Mothering by the Book*, we'll look at classic stories that shape the libraries of our homes and identify the fears that steal the joy of motherhood. We will define the ways that we have lived as if these fears of the future were present reality, and then begin to rewrite that story. As we look at these classics and identify the traits of those characters who became heroes, and the tools that guided them on their journey, we will learn to put these tools into action in our own lives so we can live out a story of hope. With the truth of Scripture refining our character toward hope and heroism in the face of fearful circumstances, we'll learn to take our thoughts captive and soak in the truth until it starts to transform us from the inside out. And then—inspired by the stories and strengthened with the Word of God—we will rip up fear by its gnarly roots and learn to live joyfully and free. We will save childhood and freedom and fun, one read-aloud book at a time.

In her book *Awaking Wonder*, Sally Clarkson remembers a time when her four-year-old daughter, Joy, confidently waved her bubble wand over and over while saying, "I am putting beauty back into the mountains like God did with the stars."[3] Joy wasn't afraid to have fun, or to make the world a better place; fear had not yet stained her life. In *Mothering by the Book*, we are working our way back to that place of little-girl hope that empowers us to change the world and love our lives, instead of staying stuck in fear.

Introduction to the Study Guide

Each chapter of *Mothering by the Book* is about a story—the tale of a fight with fear—and about the stories and the tools that helped me overcome. My goal, however, is that this is more than just a story for you. I want this to be a tool you can apply in your own life to experience more freedom and joy. For this to work, plan to set aside some time at the close of each chapter to ask yourself a few questions and let God illuminate the answers for you. As you take even a few moments to reflect and listen, God will meet you and begin to transform your heart. It would be helpful to have a special notebook for this purpose along with a quiet space. I realize that it can seem impossible to carve out quiet space and time in the busy years of motherhood, but the freedom and joy you will gain as you apply yourself to overcoming fear will be worth the energy. Stories saved my life, and my story can help you soar in your own life, and give your children wings in the process.

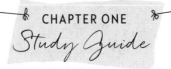

CHAPTER ONE
Study Guide

Circle your three favorite books from childhood (or write them on the following page):

Little House on the
    Prairie
Little Women
The Boxcar Children
Winnie-the-Pooh
Charlotte's Web
The Railway Children
The Yearling

The Cabin Faced West
Indian Captive
Roll of Thunder, Hear
    My Cry
The Lion, the Witch and
    the Wardrobe
Betsy-Tacy
Anne of Green Gables

Ramona   *Freedom Train*
Little Britches   *All-of-a-Kind Family*

What is one lesson you learned from these books?

Circle two things fear says to you:

- I can't manage.
- My kids will get hurt.
- I'm afraid of failure.
- People don't like me.
- I'm not smart enough to homeschool my kids.
- I'm not lovely enough to keep friends.
- The future is frightening.
- I don't have what it takes.
- I can't handle more children.
- My marriage won't make it.
- My child won't love God.

Write down any fears you have that are not on the list above.

A VERSE TO MEMORIZE

Look up the following Scripture passages and write down the one that speaks most to you: John 15:13; Romans 5:8; Romans 8:32; Romans 8:38–39; 1 John 4:7–10. Memorize the verse most meaningful for you.

Overcome the Fear of Being Alone through Journaling

LITERATURE COMPANION: *Pride and Prejudice*

Those who do not complain are never pitied.

Jane Austen, *Pride and Prejudice*

I was a child bride. I started earning money when I was twelve and started college at sixteen, but it's the bride part that really gets people. I dropped out of my public high school at the ripe age of fifteen, passing the California High School Proficiency Exam in order to break free. I had done independent studies at home as a junior high student, but I soon grew tired of the loneliness of trying to do schoolwork by myself while my mom worked full-time. Once a week, I worked with my dad in his landscaping business, mowing lawns for spending money, but most of my days were spent at home alone while my older and younger siblings went to school or to work.

Tired of this lonely life, I enrolled in public high school (where I lasted fewer than two years), dreaming it would be just like one of the silly SWEET VALLEY HIGH books that I had read as an adolescent. I thought I could waltz in there and be a cheerleader and popular, despite the fact that with my red hair, temperamental personality, and lack of money, I resembled Anne of Green Gables or Pippi Longstocking more than the boy magnet I fantasized of being. Despite these hard truths, I was a dreamer and took a chance on high school popularity.

My experience was nothing like Sweet Valley High. I couldn't afford to be a cheerleader, and while I landed a starring role in the school play—hardly a ticket to popularity—I eventually quit that in protest of having to kiss the greasy forehead of my onstage husband. I barely made it into my sophomore year before I left school altogether, weary of the humiliation of having to ask to use the bathroom after experiencing relative freedom as a junior high student. Alone. At home. Just me and my workbooks, but with the freedom to go to the bathroom or raid the fridge anytime I wished.

I think I was especially hoping that I'd find a boy to love me in high school. My parents loved me, sure, but I was the middle child, and I was like a bucket with holes. No matter how much love I got, I never really *felt* loved. On my first day of high school, I locked eyes with a tall, brown-eyed boy and fell hard. And then the next week, I fell for someone else. I spent my early teen years falling for one boy after another, until at the ripe old age of sixteen, as I made my New Year's resolutions, I gave up on dating.

Just over a month into my "no dating" phase, I was working at a local clothing store, and my manager decided to set me up with her boyfriend's best friend. I persistently said no, worn out after a short but fierce streak of promiscuity, until one day I finally ran out of excuses and said, "Fine. I will go on a blind date with your boyfriend's best friend."

We crowded into her boyfriend's pickup truck and headed to the drive-in theater. I was awkwardly perched on the edge of my date's knees because there were only three seats in the tiny truck. The movie selection was *The War of the Roses*, a film about a bitter divorce, and while I can't remember much about the movie, I do remember that my manager dumped a bucket of popcorn on her boyfriend's head, and that I fell in love.

Our courtship was brief. We started dating just after Valentine's Day, but as the days started growing warmer, and my mom noticed how inseparable we had become, she said, "You are together all the time; why don't you just get married?"

It hadn't occurred to us before that time; after all, I was only seventeen, but once my unconventional mother's words were out, we got it done. Within six months of our first date, we were married. I can remember walking down the aisle, my mouth slightly agape in shock that I was actually doing this. My friend's mom whispered as I walked by, "Shut your mouth and smile!" I composed my fearful thoughts, walked down the aisle to my husband, and we started a life together.

A Hole in My Heart

I was a very immature bride. I still burn with embarrassment that I chose the song "You Needed Me" for the candle-lighting ceremony. This seventies classic's lyrics, including "You put me high, upon a pedestal. . . . You needed me, you needed me,"[1] were so weirdly self-involved that in retrospect,

I cringe. I suppose that in light of my newfound awareness of the proclivities I face as an Enneagram 2, it makes total sense, but it's still a memory I would rather forget. At any rate, I found a man who needed me, and I needed him too. Our shared insecurities and family dysfunction created the beginnings of a story that includes plenty of joy and pain. I thought I had resolved my fears of being alone, but neither marriage, nor friends, nor children, nor anything aside from God can fill that loneliness.

Our first three years of marriage were emotionally turbulent as I worked through childish bouts of envy and one particularly distressing season when I read a romance novel a day in an effort to numb the pain of feeling unloved. It didn't seem to matter how loving my husband was—it was never enough. The hole in my heart wasn't husband shaped; I needed God to heal my fears, fill my loneliness, and help me feel loved.

We kept pressing forward in our efforts to build a Christian family, even before we had children, but we had no idea where to start. All we had was each other, but our misunderstandings and communication issues meant that we often were at odds with each other. We would always make out, make up, and muddle through, but we had a lot to learn about a healthy marriage and laying a foundation for a godly family, and my fears of being unloved were sabotaging our efforts. This fear made me mistrust my husband and try to control my circumstances, and it opened the door for pain in my children's lives caused by our marital struggles.

Fear Causes Strife

Other couples have faced the fear of being unloved, and while most of the stories presented in this book offer inspiration for overcoming fear, this one is more of a cautionary tale. *Pride and Prejudice* is a Regency novel by the prolific Jane Austen, and my daughters and I read and discussed it as part entertainment, part character training. The A&E film version with Colin Firth as the silent and mysterious Mr. Darcy became a family favorite, and my oldest daughters even had small parts in a stage version of the story. However, the book is more than just a love story. It's also a deft character study, and it speaks volumes about the impact of fear on relationships. Several couples appear in the book, including Mr. and Mrs. Bennet, Elizabeth and Mr. Darcy, Lydia and Mr. Wickham, Jane and Mr. Bingley. But one woman stands out for illustrating the harm that comes when we live in fear: Mrs. Bennet, the mother of the main characters.

Even though the story's central characters, Elizabeth and Jane Bennet, seem to have retained some self-possession, their mother is clearly a woman scorned. A woman who knows she is loved can behave with dignity; she can, as Proverbs 31:25 says, "[laugh] at the time to come." This is not so true of a woman who fears she is unloved. Elizabeth's mother, Mrs. Bennet, is full of fear: fear for her financial future, fear of shame, fear of ruin. And at the core of any lack of faith lurks the fear that nobody loves us enough to look after us. Because Mrs. Bennet fears she is unloved, she contrives to find husbands for her daughters, seeks to control her own husband, and ultimately shames them all by her meddling. Watching the movie version made me cringe with embarrassment as I watched her screech about her nerves, manipulate her daughters, and constantly work to keep herself the center of attention. She grasps desperately for love and security. I wanted to reach into the television and lovingly shake her; I wanted to wake her up to the destruction she was causing.

But we all probably can relate to Mrs. Bennet on some level. We've all been in that place where we've complained or gotten bossy with our husband or overly controlling with our children. Maybe we aren't quite as strident about it as Mrs. Bennet is, but we've all acted clingy and manipulative, or played the victim in an effort to manage our circumstances. At the root of these behaviors, we usually find fear. We'll address many fears in this book, but when we chase them all down to their source, we discover the fear that tells us we aren't loved or lovable.

This fear tells us that we are on our own. It implies that there is no one to care for us and that we must control our circumstances to be safe. This fear insists that it is entirely up to us to keep our marriages together, our children safe, and our lives predictable. Fear drives us to push those we love away, as our core beliefs that we are unlovable and that those we love will leave us incite wall-building behaviors. The worst part of living in this fear for any length of time is that it also builds up a hard veneer of bitterness. When our core belief that we are unloved manifests, it causes us to drive people away, confirming that we are unloved. Our fearful behavior causes a tumultuous cycle of craziness that makes us alternately hard and needy as we try to grasp love.

> When we chase these fears down to their source, we discover the fear that tells us we aren't loved or lovable.

But how can we convince ourselves that we are loved? God tells us he loves us; John 3:16 says he loves us so much that he sent his only Son to die for us. However, for those of us who have experienced neglect or abandonment in our own childhood, it can be hard to make the truth of Scripture translate from our head to our heart. When we had parents who were too busy to pay attention to us, when we spent a childhood playing alone, when we had parents who were constantly fighting, or when one of our parents abandoned us through a divorce, it builds up fear in our heart that we are inherently unlovable. It creates False Evidence Appearing Real, the acronym FEAR. And this false evidence that we replay in our heads—"My dad left, so my husband might leave also" or "My mom never cared about me, so I'm afraid God won't care about me either"—is what leads us into the crazy behavior we see in Mrs. Bennet. Her childish tantrums, the manipulation, and the bitterness all can be traced back to the fear that nobody loves her enough to care, so she needs to make a spectacle of herself to get her needs met.

In one particularly emotional scene, we find her wailing about her youngest daughter, Lydia, having ruined the family after she ran off with an officer without the benefit of marriage. In Regency times, for a woman to be alone with a man was enough to ruin her reputation, but to spend a night together would ruin not only her own chances of a proper marriage but the reputation of her whole family. "Mrs. Bennet . . . received them exactly as might be expected; with tears and lamentations of regret, invectives against the villainous conduct of Wickham, and complaints of her own sufferings and ill-usage."[2]

Mrs. Bennet is rightfully distressed about the situation, but the sad truth is that in her desperation to get her daughters married off, she had put Lydia in the position to make such a drastic mistake. She overrode her older daughter's better judgment in the case, and now tries to blame someone else for the results. The whole situation only serves to give Mrs. Bennet more excuses for being angry and identifying as a victim, despite her having played a part in it with her manipulation and conniving. Her core belief that she was unloved kept creating circumstances that seemed to validate this lie.

But it's not just Mrs. Bennet from *Pride and Prejudice* who faced this fear of being unloved and let it create destruction in her family. In our years of marriage ministry, we've had the honor of walking many couples through their issues, and we have seen how a person's fear of abandonment and the belief that they aren't loved pushes couples apart. It causes them to act out in an effort to guarantee their spouse's love, and in the process, they inflict trauma on their children. In turn, this makes the children feel lost and afraid, perpetuating a cycle of conflict in their future marriages and homes. As the couples tenaciously try to secure love for themselves, they accuse, place blame, and grow ever more bitter and disappointed in the process. This pattern isolates us even more from the love we need and perpetuates a vicious cycle in our children. My own behavior during our worst conflicts— screaming at my husband, slamming cupboard doors, and hiding away in my room to cry, caused trauma to my children as well, and they have the scars to prove it.

I was packing a box of my adult son's belongings one day, and his journal was on top. It "just happened" to fall open, and I furtively scanned the page, only to find that it was his journaling with God. He was writing about the impact our fights had on him when he was young and recording what he felt God was saying about the situation. God told him that even though his parents had fought and it made him feel alone and ignored, God would never leave him and was always with him. As I read his words, filled with a mix of guilt for reading his journal and hope in the current work of God in his life, I was reminded of how this simple act of grieving through journaling has helped to heal my own fearful heart.

Journaling with God has been a means of reassuring myself that I am loved. When my husband and I were in conflict, and I didn't know what to do or how to resolve it, I would open my journal and start writing. When I felt alone and afraid because of life's circumstances, I would take time to process with God by writing down what I was feeling and what I was hearing. Because I had already made knowing the Word of God a priority in my life, I knew how the Father speaks, so my journaling might be copying down Scripture verses, or it might be just letting my pen flow with the words I felt my Father was speaking to me. Journaling helped me to process what I was feeling in a way that didn't cause residual trauma to my children the way uttering things like "You don't care about me!" to my husband would have done.

It was an effective way to get clarity about a situation, but it was even more effective when I also gave myself some time to grieve. Journaling grief was the one tool that served to crack the bitter veneer and release me to experience God's love. As I poured onto the pages of my journal all the pain I felt because of the conflict and misunderstanding, as I took time to identify the events that had built these walls, God's light began to shine through. The truth that God loves me streamed over my heart as the light of his Word shone on the lies and the grief and the fear. I let the work of grief, of identifying where this pain started, break up the fallow ground of my hard and hurting heart.

The Healing Power of Grieving

The Jews have a custom of "sitting shiva" when there is a death. Instead of moving on quickly after a loss, they take the time to talk about what happened and to grieve the loss. In Christian cultures, we push forward, trying to put on a brave face and get back into life, but when we fail to grieve the great losses of our life—the loss of a parent, the loss of a dream, the loss of our own childhood even—we fail to let ourselves be loved, by God and by those around us. This rushing past pain only perpetuates the fear that we aren't lovable. Taking time to grieve is an action that implies we are human and worthy of love.

The problem with our normal operating mode, pushing onward while skipping this grief step, is that we keep ourselves locked into deeper grief that can steal our joy. The psalmist David knew the necessity of journaling his grief. He sat with God, pouring out his heart in lament: "To you, O Lord, I call; my rock, be not deaf to me, lest, if you be silent to me, I become like those who go down to the pit" (Psalm 28:1). His grief poured out, he could get back in the fight with joy restored.

When this grief washed over me and washed my heart clean, I was able to love my family again. I was able to love with a pure heart, without expectations, and without the grasping and controlling that happens when we are fearful. I let God into the hurt places, and in the process, he shone the healing light of his love on those wounds. I was molested by a farm worker as a six-year-old, and I had let that incident, along with my parents' fighting and the neglect I felt because of their busy lives, perpetuate a fear that I wasn't worth loving and protecting. When, through journaling, I let God expose those events, when I took the time to remember them, cry over them, and ultimately write a hopeful letter from God about his love for me, I was freed. The walls that I had built up around my heart broke, and joy, joy, joy was mine. No longer did the lie that I was unloved speak to me and keep me chained to fear. I wish I had known to do this much, much earlier in my journey as a mother, but it's never too late to process our pain and break free of fear.

Now I could be silly with my children without fear of shame, or take a missionary adventure into wild places without fear of injury, all because I knew that my Daddy in heaven loves me and will never leave me. Taking time to grieve opened the door to new joy, and it was the important first step in my fight to overcome my fear.

You can do this too. In future chapters, we'll tackle those specific mothering fears that need practical strategies, but if we don't first take time to grieve the ways that fear has stolen from us, no amount of practical advice will make an impact. When you pause your busy life for a moment to take stock of the pain you've already experienced, you can break free of the prison fear has created around you. You can break out of the cycle of anxious and controlling behaviors and find new joy and anticipation for your life. Grief hurts at first; it's sure to make you cry. But bitterness will break your bones, and that's the rotten fruit of just pushing through and pressing down the hurt. You can't skip the process, and the

> When, through journaling, I let God expose events, when I took the time to cry over them, and ultimately write a hopeful letter from God about his love for me, I was freed.

fear of being unloved only grows if we don't take the time to properly heal the wounds that caused it.

Once upon a time, Mrs. Bennet had been a lovely woman; the fact that she had a husband and five daughters attests to a relationship that must have had some love in it. Sadly, living with the fear of being unloved had turned her into a loudmouthed bore, and caused people to shrink away from her, which only served to affirm the lie that she was not lovable, which in turn bred more fear.

But you can have a different story. You can identify the times in your life when you felt unloved or abandoned, and as you grieve the places in your past where love seemed far away, you can let your One True Love, the God who *is* love, heal your heart. Instead of letting fear lead you into damaging behaviors that cause pain to yourself and those you love, you can sit quietly with your heavenly Father and let him comfort you and reassure you that you are safe and you are loved.

Jeremiah 31:3 tells us that God has loved us with an everlasting love. He's always been there loving us. He will take care of us, and he's patiently waiting for you to break free and experience his love. When you know you are loved, when you have overcome the fear that you aren't the beloved, then you can love your children with the pure, joyful love of Jesus. You can be a safe place for them, and in the warmth of your love, they too can overcome fear.

CHAPTER TWO
Study Guide

Take some time to journal the events in your life that have caused pain or made you doubt the love of God, or even the love of your parents.

Spend some time feeling the pain of those situations, and cry if you need to. Tears are a baptism into new joy.

Write a letter from God to yourself; let your pen flow with words of love and kindness from your heavenly Father.

A VERSE TO MEMORIZE

Write out this verse as a reminder that God is the strength of your life:

> The LORD is my light and my salvation; whom shall I fear? The LORD is the strength of my life; of whom shall I be afraid?
>
> PSALM 27:1 KJV

MORE BOOKS ABOUT
Marriage and Relationships

To Read Aloud
Love Comes Softly by Janette Oke
Belles on Their Toes by Frank B. Gilbreth Jr.
and Ernestine Gilbreth Carey

For Mom
Stepping Heavenward by Elizabeth Prentiss
Mother by Kathleen Norris
First We Have Coffee by Margaret T. Jensen

Overcome the Fear of the Baby Years by Staying Present

LITERATURE COMPANION: *Baby*

"You took a great risk," he said.
It was the first time he had spoken.
Julia looked at him, then at the rest of us.
"But that is what a mother does," she said.

Patricia MacLachlan, *Baby*

When my first pregnancy test showed the two lines, I was thrilled, ecstatically ready to conquer the world of mothering. I devoured books about pregnancy and childbirth, preparing to be the best mother ever. I ate exactly the right proportions of protein and carbs, drank pungent raspberry and nettles tea to strengthen my uterus, and walked every day as part of my training for a medication-free birth. We even practiced perineal massage, my husband stretching me with his fingers while I breathed through the pain to imitate the crown of fire when the baby's head would begin to emerge. No fun was had during these exercises, but I was sure that I could handle the difficulty of childbirth after these painful practice sessions.

It wasn't just birth that I was studying, though; I threw myself into books about parenting, full of confidence that I could train my children to be wise and happy and good. I was eager for this new adventure. But then I had actual children. And I realized that it wasn't as easy as it seemed.

My first infant would stay awake all night, and I'd be stuck pacing the floor, trying to get her to burp and fall asleep as I pondered what I was doing wrong. I tried walking faster, bouncing more vigorously, nursing more often, and adjusting her position in a desperate effort to get her to sleep before I lost my mind. My second infant projectile-vomited after every feeding, precipitating an endless search for answers to her tummy troubles. I eliminated coffee and dairy from my diet, and we burped her more frequently. We finally resorted to giving her a pacifier between feedings so at least we'd be warned when the pacifier popped out just before the flood of stinky spit-up.

With each new child came new reasons to feel afraid, as I wondered how I could meet their needs and safely get them to adulthood. Over time, the bright and excited young mother had been reduced to a deer in the headlights, wondering which way to turn and where the next pitfall would be. I started spending too much time in my head, wondering how I would meet the needs of all my children. I wondered how I could possibly manage to homeschool, feed, and care for my growing brood.

I remember one particularly tough morning when I was rudely stirred out of sleep by the pungent smell of pee from the toddler's leaky diaper. He had stealthily crawled into my bed in the wee hours, looking for cuddles and giving me a wet bed in exchange. Instead of changing those sheets immediately, I quickly washed up the sodden child, and we crawled into one of the older kids' beds. We had just snuggled in when the same dear little toddler started a coughing fit that ended with his throwing up on that bed. Now I had two huge loads of soiled laundry to get started before I could begin our morning time. I wearily stripped the beds and loaded the washing machine, then I fed the children breakfast, and we gathered for our daily morning ritual, which included reading aloud to begin our school day.

I had finally sat down in my comfy rocking chair and picked up our story when I heard a banging noise behind me. I craned my neck around to see what the disturbance was and peered at the ugly face of our billy goat staring through the window at me. He had hopped his fence and was now alternating between butting his head against my patio door and jumping onto the Ping-Pong table. Our attention diverted, I sprung from my chair to corral the furry creature, awkwardly pulling him by his two horns back to the fence while one of my boys opened gates for me and another child kept an eye on the toddler.

We finally got through our morning school time, but this day was just one of many that pushed me to my physical limits as I sought to meet the needs of my family, those nagging thoughts of not being able to manage, not getting enough schoolwork done, and not doing enough for my children plaguing my brain. Instead of savoring the baby season, I was squandering it as I let fear and worry lie to me. I was missing the beauty of my life: the bright blue eyes of my crea-tive ten-year-old as he explained a new science experiment to me, the sweet songs my twelve-year-old was learning on the guitar, and the clever play of my eight-year-old. It was all a blur. My body was there, but my mind was far away and full of worry. I wasn't savoring the present because I was worried about the future.

Sure, there were seasons when I was better at being all there. When my fourth baby was born, I had finally figured out that the scrubbing and cleaning could wait while I turned my attention to the wee ones growing so fast. I could say, in the language of the little poem I had learned, "Quiet down cobwebs, dust go to sleep, I'm rocking my baby, and babies don't keep."[1] I had begun to recognize that I wouldn't always have an infant to rock and hold. I had been working toward being more present, and I was for a while, but then I would slide back into worrying about the future, and I'd start miss-ing the joy in the present again.

During one of these worry-filled summers, I read a book aloud to my children called *Baby* by Patricia MacLachlan. In this story, a sweet baby is dropped off on the doorstep of a family, and they set out to care for the mystery infant. The whole family— mother, father, sister, grandma—get in-volved with loving and nurturing this small child, even though they had suf-fered the loss of their own infant only a year or so earlier. It was as if they had been saving up all the love they wanted to pour out on their own child and now lavishly showered it on this new baby. They sang to her, repeated her baby

> The family in *Baby* stayed present for the child despite their personal pain and confusion, and they gave her the gift of connection.

words back to her, pointed out colors and birds and the sky to her, and in every way showed her that she was wanted and loved. They stayed present for the baby despite their personal pain and confusion, and they gave her the gift of connection.

Love Equals Presence

What happens when we stay present in our own lives? We show our people that they are wanted and loved. And that is exactly what I *wasn't* doing when I was spending so much time in my head, worried about the future. It wasn't always big stuff either. The period in my life over which I have the most regrets wasn't a terrifying time; I just had so much work on my plate that I spent a lot of time wondering how I would manage it all, and who I could get to help me, and where was that child who was supposed to pick up the pile of leaves!

I missed out on a beautiful parade of boyish creativity and projects while I stayed so focused on my own work. My twelve- and ten-year-old sons were making massive Lego creations, writing books, building forts, and creating whole imaginary worlds, and I was too worried about how much laundry there was and what I would make for dinner next week to pay attention.

As mothers, we do have to spend a certain amount of time thinking and processing, but there was a cost to my family when I let my attention wander into worry. That cost was connection. When I stayed in my head, thinking about all that needed to get done or how I would meet the needs of each child, I was missing the present beauty of my children, and I was communicating to them that they weren't important enough to notice. My fear of not meeting the needs of my children caused me to not meet their needs.

In the book *Forever and Always* by Steven and Celestia Tracy, the authors point to the impact of childhood bonding and connection on healthy marriages. They write, "As children, our first sense of value was the image of ourselves we saw reflected in the eyes of our mother. Was she available, responsive, and comforting? Did she like being with us, or were we a nuisance to be 'put up with?'"[2]

And herein lie many of my own issues with fear, as well as the costly impact my anxiety was having on my children. My own mother lived in fear of the future, a fear born out of her own childhood with a World War II veteran who was suffering from undiagnosed post-traumatic stress disorder. Throughout much of my childhood, my mother was too busy worrying about the future to take time to look me in the eyes and reassure me that I was loved and that I would be okay. And I did the same thing to a few of my own children. I failed to stay present, failed to look them in the eyes and give them the gift of my undivided attention—and it cost them connection. But it wasn't an insurmountable problem, and it's never too late to turn things around.

Maybe you see yourself in this story and realize that in your fear of not managing your children, you are not loving your children. Perhaps you realize that you've been far away mentally even while physically present, letting fear keep you in your head instead of being able to savor the present. But you can write a better story, and *Baby* can help.

You see, the family in *Baby* had every reason in the world to be far away. They had lost an infant and were still mourning that loss, keeping each other shut out of their pain. But as they rallied around that little doorstep-dropped baby, their wounded hearts began to heal. As they all stayed present to each moment, whether it was a new step from the baby, a new word, or even the color of the sky, they were able to come back to their life together and truly see and love each other.

They stopped scattering in crisis, stopped letting their emotions drive them apart, and stayed in the fight for connection, even when it hurt. They did all this knowing that they probably wouldn't get to keep the baby, knowing that eventually the baby's mother would show up and they would have to let her go. They didn't worry about the pain they would face in the future. They stayed present to loving that child and let future worries go.

And this is what I began to do. As I became awake to the damage I was inflicting on my children by being physically present but mentally far away, and as I began to turn my attention back to my beautiful people, we started to heal the broken bonds. As I began to notice them in their play, taking joy and delight in their creativity, their discoveries, and even their messy process, they began to settle into feeling loved and delighted in, which sparked new creativity and new adventures. I started noticing the beautiful sunsets and the golden light resting on my children as they did one more flip on the trampoline. When they came up to the house covered head-to-toe in mud because they had literally stripped off all their clothes and rolled in a giant mud puddle, I let my first reaction be laughter before making them hose off.

I started to enjoy my children instead of merely trying to raise them, and I did this out of a realization that God enjoys us. As I began to let God into my own childhood wounds and ask for his perspective on them, I could sense his enjoyment of me as a person, and that shifted my perspective on my children. I realized that it's not enough to simply keep our kids fed and clothed. For them to be awake to the wonder of their own lives, they have to know that we don't just love them—we enjoy them.

Just as the family members in *Baby* were paying attention to that sweet infant and applauding her every move, God is paying attention to us. Psalm 139 says that we are fearfully and wonderfully made (v. 14), known, and loved by God. It goes on to say, "How precious to me are your thoughts, O God! How vast is the sum of them! If I would count them, they are more than the sand" (vv. 17–18).

He is excited about us. He longs for relationship with us. He isn't just thinking about how he can get through the job of parenting us, but he delights in us and sings over us.[3] He knows every hair on our head.[4] And he can empower us to give our children that same gift of delighting in them. God can empower us to overcome fear so that we can stay in the moment with our children. To reorder our priorities so that we can manage our family while still enjoying them. To know what is important so we aren't distracted by the trivial.

Let Go of Fear

In future chapters, as we work through more of our shared fears, we will develop strategies for hanging on to joy in the busy life of motherhood; but right here, I want to help you let go of a big fear many moms face: "I'm afraid I'm not doing enough."

There are lots of smaller fears that swirl around this one, such as, "I can't manage to teach multiple ages." "My kids won't be prepared for adulthood." "I can't meet multiple academic needs." But this overarching fear of not doing enough is a big one that drives a lack of presence. Even on a day that goes well, when everyone is happy and creative, it whispers to us and steals the joy in the moment.

But the truth is, you are enough. And if you are home-schooling, you need to know that teaching children basic academic skills doesn't need to take twelve years, so you don't need to panic if your own dear baby interrupts your morning time or if the toddler needs attention during the math lesson.

So take a deep breath in, and breathe out all of the fear, because the early years with your children can be spent reading beautiful books together, talking about them, and playing with math and recipes and nature without sacrificing either educational aspirations or the enjoyment of the baby years. In fact, Finland has a legendary school system that consistently scores high on international education assessments, and yet they don't even start formal schooling until age seven. One of the founders of Head Start, Edward Zigler, writes, "There is a large body of evidence indicating that there is little if anything to be gained by exposing middle-class children to early education. . . . Those who argue in favor of universal preschool education ignore evidence that indicates early schooling is inappropriate for many four-year-olds and that it may even be harmful to their development."[5]

Education researcher David Elkind said, "There is no evidence that such early instruction has lasting benefits, and considerable evidence that it can do lasting harm. . . . If we do not wake up to the potential danger of these harmful practices, we may do serious damage to a large segment of the next generation."[6]

These studies reiterate the fact that pushing our children beyond what is developmentally appropriate and cutting out nature study and play and music and art is unnecessary and harmful. The peaceful atmosphere of a home where Mama is relaxed and happy and not feeling pressured to measure up to the neighbors' educational aspirations is a gift to your children, both educationally and spiritually. When your children feel that home is a safe place, where the adults are present and relaxed, they can rest and learn as well. When we lay aside the weight of unreasonable expectations and the evil "race to the top" that has been imposed on our children by curriculum producers and well-meaning bureaucrats, we can savor the fleeting years with our children instead of constantly living in fear of the future.

And the years are fleeting. I have seven children, and amid the baby years, I felt like I would be changing diapers forever, that my nipples would fall off from nursing so many years consecutively, and that I would never be able to shower alone again. But the truth is, the baby years flew by. My own baby is twelve years old now, with the aroma of a hardworking man. The days of having an infant look at me as if I was the most beautiful woman in the world are long gone.

Nobody besides Jesus will adore you the same way your infants do, and this season of your life is worth savoring. It's worth marking and remembering, and taking time to smell and feel and love these years. You can't rewind once they're gone, and there is no stopping time. The best you can do is shake off the fear and let yourself live in these beautiful days. Be all here and all in. God loves you, and he delights in you, and he can help you be present in these precious days with your children.

Simple Steps to Stay Present

Practically speaking, how can we be present with babies when trying to get school-aged children educated or off to school?

How can we be attentive and give eye contact to our middle children when we are also trying to nurse and nurture an infant? It is easy to say, "Let go of fear and be present," but a little harder to practically apply those words when we are exhausted and in the thick of this crazy season.

But there are some practical things we can do.

1. Stop Looking at Our Phones

When my oldest children were infants, we didn't have smartphones, but I still squandered eye contact by reading or talking on our old corded phone. So make sure to give your babies eye contact. Look at them, listen to them, repeat back what they say. When your children talk to you, look at them and respond. We have years ahead of us when there won't be so many people needing eye contact from us, but in this short season, when our babies are learning that they have value because a parent looks them in the eyes, put aside the distractions and smile and laugh and look at your babies.

2. Simplify Meals

I taught my toddlers to get themselves a bowl of dry cereal so I could finish nursing the infant in the morning, and I kept healthy snacks such as cheese, carrots, and bananas easily accessible. I also taught children to contribute to the work of making and cleaning up meals. If we can work together on the feeding of our people, then we will all have more time to notice the beauty of our life.

3. Simplify Home Care

We don't have to decorate for every season, and it doesn't matter to our babies if their nursery is Instagram-worthy. You only get one baby season with each of your children, so keep your home simple so that relationships come first. This can still be lovely, but it doesn't have to absorb all our attention. Ask your family what helps them feel comfortable at home and curate your home for the people who actually live there.

4. Simplify School

If you are homeschooling, spend the early years doing the basics. As David Elkind pointed out in the above quote, early years schooling doesn't have to be formal, so make the focus on reading great books together, talking about what you read, and playing with math. You can wait to read *Plutarch's Lives* until all your children are ready for it (maybe that will be never), and you can make the early years of schooling focused on story and on relationships. If your children are in a traditional school, try to negotiate for reasonable homework loads with teachers, or find ways to get through assignments quickly. Children need to move and play and create; they don't need every activity of the day dictated by adults.

5. Notice the Beauty

When we work to keep our mind in the present, when we discipline ourselves to be fully here, instead of somewhere in the future, feeling scared, we can start to overcome our fear. When you notice that your mind is wandering, and you imagine your children not being able to get into college because you didn't teach them to read when they were four, or you imagine your child not being able to find a wife because he didn't get teeth brushing down when he was six, bring your attention back into the here and now. Maybe you need a little cue word or phrase; one of our counselors told us to say, "That's a lie" when we started worrying about the future.

Maybe for you, a simple breath prayer: "Jesus, come near." Whatever works for you. Just find a way to pull yourself into the present so you don't miss the beauty of this season.

It's a messy dance, trying to maintain a life while still being present with our children. I find myself struggling with being in the present even now. I've got birthday celebrations to plan and seasonal decorating to get started on, and it's amazing how simple tasks can become fear triggers as we let our imagination wander: "What if all the holiday decor is sold out, and we have the worst celebration ever?" "What if my child is disappointed with his gifts and feels unloved and starts looking for love in all the wrong places?" We mothers have such vivid imaginations, and they can take a slight worry and blow it up into a big, life-altering fear. But we can win this fight for joy. We can let go of the fear of the future and the worries that steal our peace. We can begin to see the beauty of our present life and uncover the joy and beauty in each new day. We can ask Jesus to come and be with us right now and help us stay in our lives and stay awake to the beauty around us.

> We can ask Jesus to come and be with us right now and help us stay in our lives and stay awake to the beauty around us.

Sometimes I wish I could turn back the clock for just a moment. I wish I could smell the breath of my infant after a feeding or feel the soft smoothness of their little chubby faces. I wish I could rewind and once again hear the adorable little sentences and songs strung together by my own three-year-old: "Tinkle, tinkle, ittle tar, how me, know me, where me are!" Or play Calico Critters one more time with my baby girl. But those days are gone forever, and I can't get them back by wishing. I did my best to savor them in the moment, and you just need to do your best as well. So let go of the fear and be here now. Trust that when God says, "Fear not, I am with you always,"[7] it is true, and he really will be there with you, holding you and walking you through whatever challenge each new day brings. He is good, and his love endures.

At the end of *Baby*, the mother comes back for her child, and now the family has to face the pain of loss, both in remembering the passing of their own baby and in losing the doorstep baby they cared for. Miraculously, the family finds that it hasn't destroyed them. They are finally able to name the infant they had buried, whose loss had pushed them apart, causing a fracture in their love. They are able to heal from the first loss because they stayed present with the second chance. Even though there must have been some fear there—caring for that child while knowing the mother would eventually come back for her and knowing their hearts would break yet again—they didn't let fear stop them from being all in with loving that child. They didn't let the possibility of something bad happening keep them from enjoying the precious moments they were given. They stayed present and gave themselves to love. Let's do the same. Let's give all we have to stay present with our children and love them well. We only have now.

CHAPTER THREE
Study Guide

What worries keep you from being present with your children?

How can you simplify so that you can enjoy this fleeting season?

How can knowing that God is with us help us stay present with our children?

A VERSE TO MEMORIZE

Lo, I am with you always, even to the end of the age.

MATTHEW 28:20 NKJV

53

MORE BOOKS ABOUT
the Baby Years

To Read Aloud
On the Night You Were Born by Nancy Tillman
Baby Island by Carol Ryrie Brink

For Mom
The Light Between Oceans by M. L. Stedman
Papa's Wife by Thyra Ferre Bjorn

Overcome the Fear of Failure
by Speaking Life

I'll be a friend to you. I've watched you all day and I like you.

E. B. White, *Charlotte's Web*

My second child was a mystery to me. The truth is, all children are full of mystery; we might think we've solved the puzzle, and then they go through a new developmental phase, and everything changes. Children who were the most difficult babies become the easiest of adolescents, and some who were always happy and sweet as children have callused my knees in prayer as they entered the teen and adult years. But my second child was a complex bundle of differences, the Rubik's Cube of children—and mystery and differences can be frightening.

She was born at home, and her birth was a sweet experience, if birth can ever be called that. I was cozy in my bedroom, staggering from the shower, where I let steaming hot water pour down my aching lower back, to my comfortable bed, now protected by plastic sheets and pads. I was a conscientious pregnant woman, eating careful combinations of protein and vegetables for optimal development and avoiding alcohol, sugar, and pharmaceuticals to protect my baby as she developed. Home birth was to be a new adventure for me. After my first delivery—when the hospital wouldn't admit me until my cervix dilated further, and I ended up spending the excruciating labor transition in the back of my sister's car returning to the hospital—this birth was peaceful. Calmly and quietly, my daughter slid into the world. As my husband and I lay there together, with our newborn baby cradled on my naked chest, he sighed, "How delightful."

We named her Eden, which means delight. Even then, we believed that speaking life is a powerful tool in the hands of parents. As young Christians, we had read the Bible stories emphasizing the importance of the blessing. It was so important that Jacob tricked his brother to get it, and Joseph crossed Jacob's hands to manipulate which son in his own family was blessed. We had even read *The Blessing* by Gary Smalley and John Trent and knew how powerful are the words we speak. We were aware that what we say matters, that God calls us to speak life. Proverbs 15:4 says, "A gentle tongue is a tree of life, but perverseness in it breaks the spirit." Even before we had children, we were determined to use our words to build up our children instead of tearing them down.

56

Fear Creeps In

We would be tested in this, though. I wanted to speak life over my children and myself, but fear began to creep in as they grew, and it was especially pronounced with my second child. It started during her infancy with projectile vomiting. Every time I breastfed her, just as I was burping her, the milk would come up and go shooting across the room. I was utterly bewildered by the problem and began a search that would continue for years. We took her to a local clinic to see if she had a milk allergy and checked out books from the library to find a solution. As she grew, the vomiting became less severe, but then other issues surfaced. At nearly every holiday, she was cranky and out of sorts, uncomfortable in her own skin. As she neared her first birthday, she still wasn't walking, and while she eventually passed that milestone, her speech and motor skills were delayed as well. Every normal milestone was a marathon for her. Development didn't come easily for her, and seeing her struggle fueled my own fears of failure. I was like a honey badger in my search for answers. I wasn't going to give up until I found a way to help my daughter, but I felt so lost and unsure of myself, so bewildered by the unfamiliar landscape of special needs.

When I finally discovered a book that described sensory processing disorder, my child was nine, and I'd already been searching for several years. At last, there were some answers to the issues we were facing. Until then, I'd wondered if maybe I was crazy. I could see that there were differences—articulation struggles, confusion, meltdowns over an irritating shirt tag—but the books that I could find on special needs and learning disorders described children with autism, dyslexia, or developmental delays. My child was somewhere in the middle of all of that, and the confusion led to even more fear.

It also led to believing and speaking the worst. On this long road of teaching my daughter new things, I let words spill from my mouth that I've deeply regretted. "What is wrong with you?" "Why can't you remember?" I let my tone convey my frustration and fear. I would explain to her the names of the colors: "This block is red. This block is blue. This block is yellow." Pointing to each one and naming them, I finished the lesson in colors by asking her to point to the blue one, the red one, and finally the yellow one. She could remember when I was naming them, but a second later, when I pointed to a block and asked, "What color is this one?" she couldn't tell me. At that point in her life, information would go into her brain and seemingly vanish without a trace. Learning was a long road because the information didn't stick. This only added to my fear.

I was frazzled and frustrated, pregnant with my fourth child and dealing with morning sickness. We were getting ready to move to our newly purchased country property after living in a cramped rental house, and my patience was wearing thin. Desperate to be a good mom and afraid of failure, I grew increasingly discouraged as my efforts to teach my daughter seemed to fall flat. I searched for answers, visiting speech therapists, occupational therapists, and the public library in an effort to get help for my daughter. I had felt so sure of myself as a homeschooler with my first daughter; she quickly picked up on new concepts and was a voracious reader by age eight, so my only point of comparison for what was normal was her. Comparison is never a good idea with children, but as the disparities between the two grew, so did my fear and confusion as I saw that we weren't meeting milestones.

My fear intensified when at nine years old she started having seizures. One night, I listened to my oldest talk about her day as her younger sister fell asleep on the bed next to her. As I sat there watching her sleep, her arm slowly lifted, hand clenched, and she began convulsing. Her eyes rolled to the back of her head, while mine widened in terror as I watched my precious daughter in the grip of a grand mal seizure. It seemed to last forever, but in reality it ended quickly, even as it initiated an even more desperate search for answers. The seizure was followed by several more over the course of the next few months, and we added a CT scan, EEG, and neurologist visits to our already busy life with five young children.

Up Against a Wall

Busyness itself can lead to fear as we drive ourselves to exhaustion, but sometimes in our lives as mothers, we are simply up against a wall. Babies are crying, toddlers need help finding their shoes, and school-aged kids must finish their homework. We are pushed to the edge of our endurance and left gasping for air. However, when we leave no space to process our experiences, even to grieve them, it can lead to rising anxiety levels. When we try to keep pushing through these high levels of intensity in life, we will eventually hit that wall at high speed, leading to destruction. This was exactly what was happening to me. Worry for my daughter grew, and patience was stretched thin. I was working so hard to be a great mother, but because I couldn't "fix" my daughter, I felt like a failure, initiating a cycle of fear and frustration that was often followed by a burst of angry words. At the end of this cycle, I was left feeling ashamed, wishing I could undo the damage caused by my outburst. But I loved my children, and I was fierce in my pursuit of their best, and that included reading aloud to them, even on the most difficult of days.

Taught by a Spider

The read-aloud that spoke to me in this time was an unlikely one. It wasn't about a family or a human mother, but instead was about a farmyard and a runty little pig who wanted to live. In *Charlotte's Web* by E. B. White, Wilbur comes to the terrifying awareness that he is destined for the Christmas dinner table. Fear grips the little pig as the sheep describes the fate that awaits him, but Charlotte, a nondescript gray spider, intervenes in a most unusual way. Perhaps the fate that awaits an ordinary pig is to become the Christmas bacon, but Charlotte decides to endow Wilbur with greatness, and she does it through her words. She blesses Wilbur with words and phrases including *radiant*, *humble*, and *some pig*, and she convinces the world around him that he is indeed special. When Mr. Zuckerman, the owner of the farm, first encounters Charlotte's words woven into the web, he is taken by surprise: "There can be no mistake about it. A miracle has happened and a sign has occurred here on earth, right on our farm, and we have no ordinary pig."[1]

Soon, word gets out that Zuckerman's pig is a miracle pig, and people from miles around come to see him. Wilbur becomes a regular attraction, and with his awareness of Charlotte's work on his behalf, Wilbur tries to live up to her expectations. "Ever since the spider had befriended him, he had done his best to live up to his reputation. When Charlotte's web said SOME PIG, Wilbur had tried hard to look like some pig. When Charlotte's web said TERRIFIC, Wilbur had tried to look terrific. And now that the web said RADI-ANT, he did everything possible to make himself glow."[2]

As I read this, I realized that I was letting fear speak to me instead of words of life. Charlotte could have agreed with the rest of the barnyard animals that Wilbur was just a piece of meat, but instead she changed his identity and his destiny through her words.

Words Have Power

Research confirms the power of words. In the book *Words Can Change Your Brain*, Andrew Newberg and Mark Robert Waldman write,

> By holding a positive and optimistic thought in your mind, you stimulate frontal lobe activity. This area includes specific language centers that connect directly to the motor cortex responsible for moving you into action. And as our research has shown, the longer you concentrate on positive words, the more you begin to affect other areas of the brain. Functions in the parietal lobe start to change, which changes your perception of yourself and the people you interact with. A positive view of yourself will bias you toward seeing the good in others, whereas a negative self-image will incline you toward suspicion and doubt. Over time the structure of your thalamus will also change in response to your conscious words, thoughts, and feelings, and we believe that the thalamic changes affect the way in which you perceive reality.[3]

As Wilbur received the words spoken to him by Charlotte and believed those words, his life began to change. He felt radiant and terrific, and he started behaving like a radiant and terrific pig. People around him began to believe he was special as well, and the trajectory of his life stopped hurtling toward the Christmas dinner table. As I read, I realized that when I listened to fear, it caused me to speak fearful words over myself and my child. I whispered worst-case scenarios: "Maybe she will never learn to read," and "What if I can't help her?" and "I can't do this," and these whispered words began to steal my confidence and cause me to criticize my daughter. Instead of focusing on the things she could do and speaking life over her, I let fear and negative thoughts shape the atmosphere.

There was one season shortly after we had moved to Mexico, recovered from chicken pox, and returned home from a trip—several big events in a row—when my daughter's behavior was particularly challenging. She would scream when getting her hair washed, struggle to understand what was going on around her, and melt down into uncontrollable crying when meals were delayed. My patience was worn thin, had become brittle and cracked. During this season, we were working with a neurodevelopmentalist, and she asked me to make a recording for my daughter of kind words. She told me to record myself saying things like "You are a great learner," "You are a patient person," and "You are full of good ideas." I was to play these recordings as my daughter went to sleep at night to counter the effects of frustrating days. At that point, some of these statements seemed untrue, and I felt like I was being dishonest, but God speaks life over us, and I could do that for my daughter also. He calls us fearfully and wonderfully made when we are

> As I read Charlotte's Web, I realized that when I listened to fear, it caused me to speak fearful words over myself and my child.

acting in ways that are anything but wonderful. He calls us his beloved when we are living as though we hate him. He calls us good when our behavior is very bad.

Shut Down Fear

Perhaps you have been letting fear speak to you and shape your perspective so that fearful statements spill from your mouth, statements that criticize and condemn you and the people around you. Maybe you never knew the power words have to shape your world, and you've carelessly called yourself inept and labeled your children as inadequate. Perhaps in an effort to be honest, you've cursed yourself and your children, predicting future doom based on current behavior. Maybe you've even been told that it's godly to label yourself as a wretched, sniveling worm who is unworthy of love, despite the fact that the Bible says we have Christ in us. Some of you might even have been under the impression that to speak blessings, to speak life over yourself and your children, is new age mumbo jumbo, and that if you do it, you'll be just like the flashy televangelists you've been taught to despise.

But is this truly what we learn from the Bible? Is speaking life over ourselves and our children somehow ungodly, and uttering curses over ourselves and our children the holy thing to do? I make no claims of being a Bible scholar but understanding the biblical basis for speaking life is imperative. The words we speak over our children can haunt them long into their adult years. They pick up on our attitudes and expectations, and if we let fear cripple us and cause us to curse ourselves and our children, we are perpetuating pain into the next generation.

In Romans 12:14, we are told to "bless those who persecute you; bless and do not curse them," so even when our child's behavior is driving us nuts and we feel persecuted by them, we still need to speak life over them. Even when we hate ourselves and feel like we are our own worst enemy, we still need to speak life over ourselves. In Jeremiah 29:11, God makes a declaration over his people, encouraging them with the truth that he has good plans for them: "For I know the plans I have for you, declares the LORD, plans for welfare and not for evil, to give you a future and a hope."

Spies Who Trusted God

One of the most dramatic examples in the Bible of the power of speaking life over a situation is found in the book of Numbers. The Israelites had left Egypt and were wandering in the desert, trying to get to the promised land. Numbers 13 tells us that twelve men were sent to spy out the land God had promised to give them and to report on what they found. When they got back, ten of the spies told of how frightening the land was and how impossible it would be to conquer (vv. 31–33). Two of the men, Joshua and Caleb, had an opposite report, telling of the goodness of the land, that it was abundant with milk and honey and fruit; they told the people not to be afraid, that God was with them and that they could overtake the land (vv. 26–30).

Both descriptions were likely true. It all depended on perspective. Two of the spies believed that God was good and that he was for them, and they expected a good outcome. The other ten assumed the worst about God and described the dark side of the situation. Both sets of men were likely speaking the literal truth, but only one of the perspectives was genuinely true, and only one pleased God, as we see in Numbers 14:36–38: "And the men whom Moses sent to spy out the land, who returned and made all the congregation grumble against him by bringing up a bad report about the land—the men who brought up a bad report of the land—died by plague before the LORD. Of those men who went to spy out the land, only Joshua the son of Nun and Caleb the son of Jephunneh remained alive."

We might feel that we are just being honest when we tell the ugly truth about ourselves and our children. There might be a time and a place for acknowledging our failures so that we can get the help we need, but when we constantly curse ourselves and our children, speaking figurative death over the people we love most—"You are so stupid," "Don't be so lazy!" or "You are a brat!"—we don't agree with God. When God called Aaron and his sons to be priests for him, he instructed Moses to bless them, saying, "The LORD bless you and keep you; the LORD make his face to shine upon you and be gracious to you; the LORD lift up his countenance upon you and give you peace" (Numbers 6:24–26). God has made it very clear in Proverbs that "death and life are in the power of the tongue, and those who love it will eat its fruits" (Proverbs 18:21). We are called to *agree* with God and to speak life over ourselves and our children. We are called to speak blessings.

Charlotte Saved Wilbur with Words

Words were also a matter of life or death for Wilbur. If Charlotte hadn't been standing in the gap for him, speaking life over him, Wilbur's destiny would have been much different. He would have just been an ordinary, dirty little pig destined for the smoker. Her willingness to call him up to a higher place, to believe and speak better things for him, saved his life. "Mr. Zuckerman took fine care of Wilbur all the rest of his days, and the pig was often visited by friends and admirers, for nobody ever forgot the year of his triumph and the miracle of the web."[4]

So often we are at a loss about how to bless our children and ourselves. We may agree that it sounds like a good idea and that speaking life can be an antidote to fear, but we are so overwhelmed and scared that we lack the practical path to blessing. These five tips can help you get started.

1. Hold Your Tongue

The first thing to do is simply to commit to not speaking curses over your children or yourself. When we understand that words have power, that we act on the words we speak over ourselves, and when we comprehend that our children internalize the words of their parents and then live toward the identity spoken over them, we will stop letting careless words leave our mouths. "Let no corrupting talk come out of your mouths, but only such as is good for building up, as fits the occasion, that it may give grace to those who hear" (Ephesians 4:29).

We should take that to heart and keep negative thoughts and words unsaid. In the marriage ministry that my husband and I facilitate, we have seen countless couples struggling to believe they are loved or capable as adults because of careless curses their parents spoke to them. Often those negative labels become part of our self-talk, and in scary times we repeat them, causing even more fear. This doesn't mean that we can't give feedback, but there's a big difference between "Johnny, your room isn't clean yet. Please finish putting away your toys," and, "Johnny, you are such a lazy little brat! Why can't you ever clean your room properly?" The first way is instructive; the second is a curse. We do the same thing to ourselves. "Nobody came to the moms' night, so everybody hates me, and I'm a social pariah." This is much more destructive than "Nobody came to the mom's night, so God must have known I needed some quiet time." We can give feedback, but instead of framing it as "you are" statements that assault identity, let's build each other up.

2. Create Blessing Rhythms

In Jewish families, a blessing is spoken over the children at every Friday night meal; the father often lays his hands on each child's head as he blesses the child to be like Ephraim and Manasseh, or like Sarah, Rebecca, Rachel, and Leah. This calling forth of the child to follow in the footsteps of Bible heroes, followed by a whispered word of blessing about the child's own life, is a weekly rhythm that compounds into an identity of preciousness. A child who is regularly told that they are special will live out that identity. Maybe you could make a weekly commitment to say ten nice things to yourself and your children. Perhaps you have a special family meal each week during which you go around the table stating something you love about the person sitting next to you. Or you could write a weekly love note to yourself and your family members, sharing ways that you saw them shine that week. When you make a rhythm of blessing, it becomes part of the fabric of your family and empowers each of you to rise above fear and live free.

3. Create a Blessing Recording

When I started playing the voice recording for my daughter, telling her each night that she was capable, lovely, and calm, she began living up to this new identity. Similarly, when we begin to be gracious to ourselves and daily declare that we are loved and cared for, we combat fear. Fear is the belief that we are unsafe, and when we know in the core of our being that we are loved, we can overcome fear (see 1 John 4:18).

It might feel awkward at first; it might even feel as though you are lying: *How can I record myself saying that I am lovely when I feel ugly?* Or, *How can I record myself calling my child a kind and loving person when he picks fights with his siblings all day?* But God calls us "fearfully and wonderfully made" at the same time that we can see no loveliness, and He called man "good" even though man would go on to eat the forbidden fruit and ruin everything. So I think we can call out the gold in ourselves and our children. God called the whole world into existence by the word of his mouth, and we have his Spirit living in us. We can agree with God and speak life over ourselves and our family.

4. Speak the Word of God

I regularly speak a blessing over my children, taking my cue from the book *Blessing Your Spirit* by Sylvia Gunter and Arthur Burk. Even when we aren't standing right next to each other, I pray scriptural blessings over my family. "I bless you, Scott, Jennifer, Emelie, Eden, Elias, Ethan, Emmett, Ella, Ezra, to walk worthy of the calling to which you were called. I bless you to hate evil and love righteousness. I bless you to love the Lord with all your heart and soul and mind. I bless you with the peace of God that passes understanding." As my children have grown and married, I include their spouses in the prayer as well. By regularly praying and speaking Scripture over our children, we align ourselves with what is true, not with the chaos that may be happening around us.

5. Write Letters to Yourself from God

The last thing I do, and perhaps the most powerful, is to write letters to myself from God. I start out the letter with "Dear Jenny," and then just let the pen flow. God was always speaking to his people in the Bible, and I want him to talk to me also. As I write, I get direction for the days ahead and affirm his love for me. It was an awkward practice at first; my low opinion of myself and fear of misrepresenting God inhibited me, but as I've made this a regular practice, it has become a celebration. I love him, and he loves me, and his desire to dwell with his people is evident everywhere in Scripture. Lloyd John Ogilvie writes in *When You Need a Miracle*, "To be a blessed person is to know, feel, and relish God's affirmation and assurance, acceptance, and approval. It is the experience of being chosen and cherished, valued and enjoyed." [5] When we know the Word of God, we will recognize the voice of God, while the voice of a stranger we will not follow.

In that troubled season of my life, when I was overwhelmed with childhood seizures and learning disabilities while still trying to care for several younger children, I was afraid we wouldn't make it through. I imagined worst-case scenarios, like the seizures growing more regular, my child never being able to read, and the meltdowns continuing forever, but none of those scenarios happened, and we did make it through. My daughter eventually learned to read, the seizures stopped, and she grew to become one of my most patient and calm children, a beloved friend and helper.

Early in *Charlotte's Web*, when Wilbur arrives at the farm and has to be away from his first friend, Fern, Charlotte notices him and chooses him, saying, "I'll be a friend to you. I've watched you all day and I like you."[6]

> When we agree with God that we are loved and lovable and start speaking life over ourselves and our children, fear has nowhere to land.

Right from the beginning, her words convey blessing, identity, and life. I believe that God is saying the same thing to us: "The LORD your God is in your midst, a mighty one who will save; he will rejoice over you with gladness; he will quiet you by his love; he will exult over you with loud singing" (Zephaniah 3:17). God loves us, celebrates us, and calls us his own, and when we agree with God, when we agree that we are loved and lovable, and start speaking life over ourselves and our children, fear has nowhere to land. We can be a Charlotte to our children, empowering them to fight their own giants as we use our words to bless them. And we can be a Charlotte to ourselves, labeling ourselves as radiant and capable in the sacred journey of motherhood.

CHAPTER FOUR
Study Guide

What words were spoken over you as a child?

If they are good words, hold on to them. If they are negative, give them to God and ask him for new ones.

What words do you speak over your children?

If they haven't been life-giving, express your remorse to your child and ask them to forgive you. This is a beautiful way to neutralize the effects of careless words.

What words do you want to speak over yourself and your children?

Make a recording of these words and play it for yourself and your children. Here is an example: "Jenny, the Lord bless you and keep you. The Lord make his face shine on you and give you peace. Jenny, you are a gift and a treasure. You are loving and kind. You are patient, and you show perseverance in your life. You care for others, and you are diligent in your work."

A VERSE TO MEMORIZE

The LORD your God is in your midst,
a mighty one who will save;
he will rejoice over you with gladness;
he will quiet you by his love;
he will exult over you with loud singing.

ZEPHANIAH 3:17

MORE BOOKS ABOUT
Speaking Life Through Words

To Read Aloud
Seeds and Trees by Brandon Walden
Extra Yarn by Mac Barnett
Words and Your Heart by Kate Jane Neal

For Mom
The Blessing by John Trent and Gary Smalley
Words Can Change Your Brain by Andrew Newberg
and Mark Robert Waldman
All Along You Were Blooming
by Morgan Harper Nichols

Overcome the Fear of My Children Being Behind through Balance

LITERATURE COMPANION: *Understood Betsy*

You aren't any grade at all, no matter where you are in school. You're just yourself, aren't you? What difference does it make what grade you're in?

Dorothy Canfield Fisher, *Understood Betsy*

Homeschooling was something that caught my fancy from the early days of parenting. I was delighted with the idea that I could be the one to read to my children and share a love of learning with them. Together, we could create and experiment and research and grow. I was initially so sure of myself as a mom, and despite my lack of teaching experience, I embarked excitedly on the journey of teaching my own children. I attended my first Charlotte Mason homeschool group when my oldest was just three, learning about truth, goodness, and beauty from *The Charlotte Mason Companion* by Karen Andreola. I was eager to get started, and I can still vividly recall those first homeschool days with my oldest child. Some of these early lessons are treasured memories, and the activities we engaged in shaped our lives.

As part of our science learning, we cared for chickens, drew and painted birds, and planted a garden, marveling as the green shoots pressed their way through the dirt. While her two tiny siblings played nearby, we sat at a little table and learned our letter sounds, followed by filling a paper with animal stickers and counting how many we used. We read picture books and chapter books, we counted and measured, and I savored every experience as a new homeschool mom. I remember finger-painting with my daughter and feeling the squishy cool paint as we smeared it on slick white paper, or baking bread together and inhaling the unequaled aroma of yeasty loaves as they baked. Every moment of those early years of homeschooling was a delight, and I followed the parent guides, doing my best not to miss a lesson.

Homeschooling was easy and fun with just one child, and fear had no hold on me.

That is, until I added siblings to the mix. Suddenly it felt like an accelerated game of Whac-A-Mole. I'd help one child with a math problem, and then another would be crying for help. The toddler would tip over the plate of freshly cut apples, and I'd frantically pick it up, only to discover that the baby had a poopy diaper. The intensity of my children's needs began to open the door to the fear that I wasn't doing enough and that my children would all slip behind. Would they end up illiterate and aimless instead of Nobel Prize–winning missionaries as I'd once hoped?

I began to feel inadequate as the realization that I couldn't give every child individual lessons started to sink in. Whole school days were missed as I recovered from having a baby or we moved to a new home. I had such high ideals for my homeschool, but ideals and reality aren't always a match. As we added more children to our family, along with the intense daily therapies we were doing with our delayed learner, my vision of a "perfect homeschool" became a mere figment of my imagination. My dream of doing crafts every day, and completing every lesson in our books felt as out of reach as climbing Mount Everest.

While my ideals for daily crafts and lessons were dying, reading aloud was a constant. The book *Understood Betsy* gave me a welcome new perspective on learning. I had been wearing myself out trying to meet every need of my children, to be emotionally present with each of them, and to give them a magical education. I had grown up as the middle child of five, and often felt invisible, as a kid, so I was determined that all of my children would feel loved and affirmed. I studied the art and science of parenting and homeschooling to make sure I was doing it "right." Fear that my children wouldn't be prepared for life drove me to research and learn.

In *Understood Betsy*, I could see myself reflected in Aunt Frances, and it wasn't a pretty sight. Betsy was an orphan who was placed in the care of Aunt Frances, an unmarried woman with no children of her own. She took this care very seriously:

> They had given themselves up to the new responsibility, especially Aunt Frances, who was conscientious about everything.

> As soon as the baby came there to live, Aunt Frances stopped reading novels and magazines, and re-read one book after another which told her how to bring up children. She joined a Mothers' Club which met once a week. She took a correspondence course from a school in Chicago which taught mother-craft by mail.[1]

I understood how Aunt Frances felt. I, too, had poured myself into researching motherhood and education so I could do well by my children. I could understand Aunt Frances's determination to care for Elizabeth Ann with all that she was. She was trying to parent her from her own brokenness. In a later chapter, we will talk more about the danger of parenting as a reaction to how we were parented—the way Aunt Frances was trying to make up for the lack of nurture she perceived in her own childhood by being a perfect parent to Betsy. I could relate to this; while my parents did their best, there were holes. Now that I've been a mom for twenty-seven years, I realize that there will always be holes, and that my parents actually did a pretty good job. But as a young mom who thought she knew everything, all I saw were the holes. And I was not going to let there be holes in my children's lives.

Impossible Standards

Can you see what an impossible standard I was setting for myself and my children? Can you relate to wanting so badly to parent perfectly and to give your child a perfect education? Have you seen how fear takes hold as you come up against your own inadequacies? This question *Am I doing enough?* seems to haunt us, especially those of us who choose to homeschool. Even when our kids are in regular school, we can feel doubt about our choices. *Maybe I should be homeschooling?* or *Maybe my child would do better in private school?* or *Maybe a public school with more resources would be a better fit?* We want so badly to give our children our best, but fear is contagious; if our children catch it, their confidence will sink as well.

It was embarrassing to see myself so clearly in Aunt Frances of *Understood Betsy*. All the overbearing sympathy, the indulgence of every emotion the child felt, and the over-attention had caused Betsy to be very fearful, a nervous little hypochondriac. Thankfully, I had seven children to absorb my efforts, so none of them were as indulged in emotion as Betsy was, but they certainly picked up on my lack of confidence and desperation to do things perfectly. For some, that made them try harder, and for others, not at all.

> We want so badly to give our children our best, but fear is contagious; if our children catch it, their confidence will sink as well.

Things changed for Betsy, and they can change for us as well. When one of the aunts caring for her became ill, they were forced to send her away to Vermont, where a distant set of relations lived in quiet obscurity on a small farm. It was the last place the fussy Aunt Frances wanted to send Betsy. She had been aghast at the way the Putneys had treated another set of children they'd taken in: "The children had chores to do . . . as though they had been hired men!"[2] Aunt Frances didn't want Betsy to face such horrors too.

However, life with the Putneys was anything but horrible, and the contrast between fear-based parenting and fearless parenting was stark. It was as if the whole Putney community was in on this practical parenting philosophy, and as Betsy learned how to live without the weight of fear pressing down on her, she flourished.

But what was the magic that was the Putneys in Vermont? What was the difference that helped Betsy flourish instead of continuing as a frightened hypochondriac who spent her days indulging in every emotion? I believe three essential mindsets can help us overcome our own battle with parental fears.

Confidence Is Key

The Putneys were confident. Perhaps it was the fact that they lived on a farm, had raised children and animals already, and had some life experience that helped breed this confidence. The Putneys weren't flustered over every little mistake, and neither were they moved by every new philosophy. Some might have even called them simple, but their quiet confidence as they cared for each other and their community, their appreciation for beauty as they admired the poetry of Sir Walter Scott, and their knowledge of the history of their hometown displayed their wisdom. Sometimes in our search for the perfect way to parent, or the best way to homeschool, we lose sight of the essentials and create more fear in the process. It's great to do your research and to do your best to be informed about the way you are raising and educating your children, but at the end of the day, we need to recognize that there may not be a perfect way.

Some families may flourish as "unschoolers," letting children choose their own learning each day, while for others that would be chaos. Some families thrive in a rigid private school environment, but for others that only stifles creativity. What each of us needs is the confidence to know our family and to choose what is best for our children. Our children don't need a perfect method; they need to feel that we know what we are doing. When we are constantly trying new methods, whether it is a homeschool philosophy or a parenting style, it creates confusion. Our lack of confidence and our inconsistency cause insecurity in our children, providing another way for fear to slither in.

Maybe you have already struggled with this and have seen the results of it. Perhaps you have switched schools every year, bought a new math curriculum every month, and tried out every homeschool philosophy—one year reciting facts every day for Classical Conversations' memory work, and the next year making bread and knitting with Waldorf. It's okay to try new things, and even to *tidal homeschool*, switching between a more rigorous and a more laid-back homeschool style as the season dictates, but if what is underlying all of these changes is fear, your children will pick up on that and miss out on the beauty of what they are learning.

I have struggled with this. I am not a naturally consistent person, and love for my children and desire to raise them well can cause me to be moved by fads. When all my friends and family were doing Classical Conversations, I was tempted to try that, even though at the time it was a terrible fit for us. When all the cool moms had their kids in sports, I wanted to put my kids in sports, even though they are not high on our family priority list. What has helped make up for my inner inconsistency and fear of missing out (FOMO) has been a clearly defined list of family essentials that created guardrails to protect our family as I worked toward confidence. In his book *Essentialism*, Greg McKeown says this about the power of knowing your essentials: "Essentialism is not about how to get more things done; it's about how to get the *right* things done. It doesn't mean just doing less for the sake of less either. It is about making the wisest possible investment of your time and energy in order to operate at your highest point of contribution by doing only what is essential."[3] We identified our family essentials and have created a template to help you identify yours as well. (Download a free family vision template at www.thepeacefulpreschool.com/blog /creating-a-family-vision.)

Becoming aware of my essentials helped me develop confidence and kept me consistent with my true values. Instead of moving from one educational method to the next in an effort to do things perfectly, we were able to stick to what was most important to our family: reading aloud, writing, basic math, nature study, and music. I knew myself and my family well enough to know that while we could do anything we wanted, I didn't have to try to make my children the best at everything. We could focus on our essentials, and if my children grew up and decided on different essentials for themselves, they would have the tools to pursue them. We took the time to understand what we loved and what was life-giving for us, and we tailored our education to those subjects instead of constantly being moved by what other people were doing.

How can you develop the confidence to stay consistent with your own values? How can you overcome the fear of not doing enough and the fear that your children will fall behind? Sometimes it is just the fruit of experience. Even the fictional Putneys might not have always been so sure about what they were doing, but I think we can jump-start confidence by identifying our essentials and letting them be a border for us. Taking time to define what is important to you can be the hedge that keeps you on the best path for your family. Knowing our essentials is one of the bricks we can use to wall out fear.

Educational Competition Isn't the Goal

When Betsy arrived at the Putney home in Vermont, her school situation changed as well. Instead of being in a large city school with modern methods of teaching, she went to a country school with all the grades together in one room. Betsy was shocked to discover that the teacher really didn't care about grades. She placed Betsy with the seventh-grade students for reading, the second-grade students for spelling, and the third-grade students for math. The important thing was learning what you needed to learn. It wasn't about competition, and there was no label applied if you seemed ahead or behind. You weren't learning disabled or gifted just because of one area of ability. You just kept learning, with no shame or acclaim attached.

Our public school system is so much different now, and it is no wonder that fear takes hold. Children are pushed harder than ever in the early years, labeled more quickly, and medicated to get through the pressure of an unnatural situation. In his book *Weapons of Mass Instruction*, former New York State Teacher of the Year John Taylor Gatto writes about school, "The rigid stupidities of forced schooling, its linear logics, its bell curves, its buzzers and tests and multiple humiliations, its resort to magical spells, fills me with rage these days as an old man. Real education can only begin out of a foundation of self-awareness. Know the truth of yourself or you are nothing but a pathetic human resource. Your life will have missed its point."[4]

Throughout Gatto's work you find a similar theme. Modern education has been created to make us fearful. It's designed to make us insecure so that we will happily bend to a consumeristic society, fitting ourselves into it as cogs in a wheel. While many of us may need to utilize the public schools, if we are aware that the focus on grades and achievement is counterproductive to actual learning, we can combat the fear of failure and resist being molded. Instead of asking ourselves, *Am I doing enough?* or *What if my child falls behind?* we should be asking ourselves, *What questions does my child have about life?* and *What work could my child take on?*

Ainsley Arment's book *The Call of the Wild and Free* tells of the first months after her son started regular school. "It wasn't long before I noticed some changes in my firstborn. His disposition toward us changed. He seemed more distant. He became more interested in what other kids thought of him. He was losing his childlike innocence. I saw the light go out in his eyes."[5]

She made the brave decision to pull him from a competitive school environment, where by all external standards he was thriving, because she saw that the competition was killing his soul.

Gatto addresses comparison and the difference in learning speeds in his book. "David learns to read at age four; Rachel, at age nine: In normal development, when both are thirteen, you can't tell which one learned first—the five-year spread means nothing at all. But in school, I label Rachel 'learning disabled' and slow David down a bit, too."[6]

According to Gatto and other researchers, the competition in schools and the drive to teach children earlier isn't yielding better results. In fact, Peter Gray's article in *Psychology Today* cited a study that exemplified this.

One study, directed by Rebecca Marcon, focused on mostly African American children from high-poverty families. As expected, she found—in her sample of 343 students—that those who attended preschools centered on academic training showed initial academic advantages over those who attended play-based preschools; but, by the end of fourth grade, these initial advantages were reversed: The children from the play-based preschools were now performing better, getting significantly higher school grades, than were those from the academic preschools.[7]

In the article referenced above, Gray cites another study that followed children into their adult years. The study found that those children who were pushed toward academics at the expense of play in the early years ended up with not only lower academic ability, but also worse outcomes in social-emotional skills. The lack of time to play and interact as young children had cost them necessary skills as adults.[8]

When we let fear drive us to push our children academically, there is a steep price to pay. Childhood shouldn't be a competition, and nobody wins when we make it so. In *Understood Betsy*, when Betsy comes home with a bad grade because she got flustered, this is her cousin's response: "'Oh, well,' said Cousin Ann, 'it doesn't matter if you really know the right answers, does it? That's the important thing.'"[9]

She wasn't dismayed because Betsy received a poor grade. She wasn't in a competition with the neighborhood to see whose kids were the most intelligent, and she wasn't going to let Betsy get into that kind of competition either. Learning was a process, not a race.

We would do well to remember this. We want our children to fulfill their God-given purpose, not win an arbitrary

> We want our children to fulfill their God-given purpose, not win an arbitrary contest that has no real purpose other than to make us all feel deficient.

contest that has no real purpose other than to make us all feel deficient. There is a saying that "'A' students go on to become professors, while 'B' students go on to work for 'C' students."[10] Though this may or may not be accurate, it highlights the fact that the skills necessary for getting good grades (compliance and attention to detail) may not be the same skills needed to think outside the box and be creative, to be leaders in business and culture. When we grade ourselves and our children, we breed fear instead of creativity. Instead, let's keep learning together. Let's shake off the fear and competition that steals our joy, that makes us question whether we are doing enough or if we are falling behind, and just seize learning as a beautiful adventure.

Learning Is a Lifestyle

The Putneys invited Betsy into the balanced life they were already living. There was a welcome mat laid out for living, and the realization that learning happens everywhere. When they churned butter, they included Betsy in that process, her aunt laughing as she recalled how her own grandmother had taught her how to handle butter. Connections were being made in Betsy's brain as she contemplated the long history that had passed in that family:

> "Why! There were real people living when the Declaration of Independence was signed—real people, not just history

people—old women teaching little girls how to do things—
right in this very room, on this very floor—and the Declaration of Independence just signed!"

To tell the honest truth, although she had passed a very
good examination in the little book on American history
they had studied in school, Elizabeth Ann had never to that
moment had any notion that there ever had been really and
truly any Declaration of Independence at all.[11]

You see, for the Putneys, education was a conversation, and
when we make education a conversation instead of a competition, children remember what they learned. Gatto writes,

In a complex society, flexible people survive best, but school—
think of the word itself—rewards rigid, miserable rule-
followers. To be effective and remain independent we need
to know how to find things out, how to manage our own
learning, but the day prison model school discourages learning for its own sake. Actual learning leads directly to low test
scores. Whatever education happens in school happens despite
school, not because of it.[12]

And Betsy was learning—she learned how to make butter,
and show compassion, and care for animals. She learned to
read aloud to bring enjoyment to others, and sew to help a
friend in need, and build community. She was learning in her
one-room schoolhouse, but she was also learning at home;
neither learning environment was elevated at the expense
of the other. Such a balanced outlook can be a great antidote to fear. As parents, we so often put "school learning"
on a pedestal, assuming that if our children aren't getting
good grades, or excelling in school, they are destined to be
destitute. We make an idol of education and in the process

rob our children of the real learning that happens in a balanced life. When we reject fear, and if necessary, reject the school systems that breed that fear, we can save childhood and empower our children to be courageous.

Success in school doesn't necessarily correlate to success in life, so instead of being afraid that our children will fall behind, let's break free of those fears and give them a whole life. Let's involve them in community service, cooking, and great conversations. Let's observe what they love to do and give them opportunities to try new things. Let's pursue our own passions and involve them in the process. Helping our children learn basic skills isn't as scary as it sounds. In fact, former Berkeley professor of education William Rohwer said, "All of the learning necessary for success in high school can be accomplished in only two or three years of formal skill study."[13]

It's easy to test out this theory in conversations with kids who were homeschooled. I've met hundreds of homeschool graduates, and while all of them had a different school experience and were fitting education into the life of the home, they have all become successful adults. I've even seen this with my own adult children. We were missionaries during some of their formative school years, which meant there were many missed school days because we were moving, or hosting groups, or building our house. School fit into our life; it wasn't our whole life, but learning was happening all the time.

I think this experience is part of what helped me overcome fear. My daughter did very little formal high school, and yet she scored above average on the SAT, graduated summa cum laude, and went on to study for a degree in law. My son missed many days of elementary school because he was helping my husband build an orphanage in Mexico, and he only did school part-time in high school because he was working for a contractor, but he also graduated summa cum laude from a local university. Learning is just what our children do, and when we don't stifle it through fear, we can let them bloom into the creative and courageous people they were meant to be. We can enjoy the process instead of squandering it, quaking in fear. Fear paralyzes us, and it makes shadows—flimsy, unimportant things—seem bigger than they are. Your child can't remember their letter sounds at age four? Just a shadow. Your child isn't reading yet at age seven? It's just a shadow and is no indication of their future success in life. Your child fails a math test? Just a shadow, trying to make you afraid, but of no real consequence. Shadows can look scary, but the truth behind them is often small and completely benign.

So let's stop asking *Am I doing enough?* and start living. Let's read books together and bake bread. Let's start businesses and gardens and involve our children in our own adventures. Let's recapture childhood by rejecting competition and believing the truth that we are capable of guiding our children to adulthood. Let's reject comparison and enjoy the short and sweet days of this journey with our children.

At the end of the book, Betsy, now a confident and caring leader, becomes aware of the fear that is driving Aunt Frances. As a baby calf approaches them, Aunt Frances panics, but Betsy, with her newfound authority, simply sends it away. This is what we can do as well. When these fears that we aren't doing enough approach us, let's call them out for the shadows they are, the inconsequential threats, and let's send them on their way. Let's take authority over our fears and self-doubt and step into a beautiful, balanced life with our children.

CHAPTER FIVE
Study Guide

The Putneys' confidence was partly due to knowing what was important, knowing their essentials. Write down a list of what you want your children to know.

Think back on your own education. Did you know everything there was to know when you graduated from elementary school? From high school?

Think about friends and family. Have you seen people become successful adults who struggled in school? Did a bad grade have the final say on their success in life?

Take some time to observe your children and note what they are learning when you aren't directly instructing them.

Write down five things you would like to learn as a family.

A VERSE TO MEMORIZE

According as his divine power hath given unto us all things that pertain unto life and godliness, through the knowledge of him that hath called us to glory and virtue.

2 PETER 1:3 KJV

MORE BOOKS ABOUT
Confidence in Education

To Read Aloud
These Happy Golden Years by Laura Ingalls Wilder
Carry On, Mr. Bowditch by Jean Latham

For Mom
Dumbing Us Down by John Taylor Gatto
The Brave Learner by Julie Bogart
Mere Motherhood by Cindy Rollins
The Call of the Wild + Free by Ainsley Arment

Overcome the Fear of Children Leaving the Faith through Family Identity

LITERATURE COMPANION: *All-of-a-Kind Family*

The children stood around the table watching her. A lovely feeling of peace and contentment seemed to flow out from Mama to them.

Sydney Taylor, *All-of-a-Kind Family*

We strolled down the dusty street, carefully balancing our candles as we tried to sing along. The Christmas carol was familiar, but we had only arrived in Mexico a few weeks earlier, so the Spanish language was still foreign, and wrapping our tongues around the new sounds was arduous. It was dark and chilly, not the cold we experience in the Northern California mountains, but the damp cold that blows over the Baja Peninsula in winter. I cuddled my children close as we balanced the candles and continued down the street, singing as we went. I was happy.

We had moved to Mexico to be missionaries, and this felt purposeful; the opportunity to reach out to the neighborhood with the invitation to join us for *pan dulce* and *champurrado* felt like real mission work. Up to that point, we had spent our days trying to navigate a new culture and language. Everything was hard. Setting up our utilities, finding a grocery store, understanding the money exchange, all the details of settling into a new place were made doubly difficult by the language barrier. But seeing the smiles on my children's faces as they experienced their first Christmas outreach in Mexico and knowing that we were part of introducing people to Jesus made the small struggles worth it.

When we moved to Mexico, our fifth child had just turned two. I had so many fears about that move. I was worried about our children's health and safety, worried about their social development, worried about their missing out on an all-American life, and worried about their going without. But as much as I was fearful, I was also hungry for God, and I didn't want to miss him. With great fear and trepidation, I was willing to leave my home and my extended family, culture, and comforts so our family could be closer to God. I knew that God is everywhere, but it can be harder to see him when we stay in our comfort zone. We wanted our children to see faith in action, because my greatest wish is that my children would know God and love him.

When I asked moms to describe their greatest fears as mothers, many of you said that your children walking away from God was the one thing you most feared, and while I believe we moms have many fears in common, if I'm afraid of my children leaving the faith, it's a fear that's hiding in the closet, behind all the others. However, I've been in many battles with the fear of my children living contrary to the Word of God. I'm desperate for my children to live close to God and am fierce about protecting them, but when fear drives our decisions, we create an atmosphere that invites opposition. It's as though we are putting up a green light for the devil to come and harass us.

The fear of our children living in sin is a common one, and it's especially pronounced in homeschool families. Some of us were wild in our teen years, and our motivation to home-school is a mix of wanting something better for our children and a desire to protect them from what we went through. I know that is the truth for me. I genuinely think I can give my children a better education than the public schools, but I also want to protect them. I want my children to be un-encumbered by the guilt and pain of adolescent mistakes. I want them to stay pure and free and innocent.

My own teen years were flagrant, and it's painful to recall some of the desperate situations I fell into. At fourteen I was drinking too much at a high school toga party. At fifteen, I was in a hot legs contest at a nightclub, shaking my under-aged booty for a bunch of drunks. At sixteen, I went to a dance club after slamming down vodka and ended up being raped in a stairwell. By the grace of God, I remembered that he existed, and that he loved me, and I disentangled myself from that messy and depraved lifestyle. By the time I was seventeen, I was married and attending church with my new spouse. But these are the kinds of memories I don't want my children to have to work through and the situations that, because of my own lack of innocence, have caused fear and pain in my life as a mother. I don't want my children to go through this pain, and I'm sure many of you feel the same way.

Tradition as an Anchor

There is a way out of this panic and a way to put up healthy fences without fear. I discovered it as I read aloud to my children. In the book *All-of-a-Kind Family*, the Jewish teachings and traditions serve as an anchor for the family, keeping them tightly connected despite the storms that come.

Reading about the weekly Sabbath preparations Mama made with her children reminded me that the Jews have been celebrating the Sabbath since the time of Moses, and many are still steadfastly keeping these traditions. Other cultures have risen and fallen, other religions have come and gone, but there is a staying power built into Jewish culture that we would be wise to understand and emulate.

As Americans, especially those of us who went through public school, we've been taught to blend in and fit in. In the process, many of us have lost our tribe of origin and the cultural anchors that provide security. We want to pass on values to our children, afraid of their choosing a different path, but so often we aren't even clear about what values we want to pass on. So many of us had families who didn't really have a culture or tradition. They went to work, they watched television, some of them maybe even went to church, but they didn't pass on traditions. There wasn't a set of standards that we were taught to identify with and to follow, and as parents ourselves, we are left anchorless and afraid, a boat in a wild sea with nothing to keep us from drifting. Others of us felt that our parents were too legalistic and the family life too rigid, so we've discarded the beauty of tradition with the bathwater of legalism, ending up with nothing to hold on to.

My parents certainly tried. We went to church every Sunday when I was a child, and I experienced the presence of God at that church. I knew him, and I loved him, but the pastor didn't represent him well, and by the time we left that church, my parents were wounded and struggled to connect back into a church community. The remainder of my childhood years were spent without the strong hedge of church and extended family community. We didn't have the ritual of weekly family rest days; we didn't have neighbors or extended family to help us stay on track. There was nothing to stop us from going off the rails when my parents, weary after carrying my brother through a bout of childhood cancer, gave in to our teenage angst.

In *All-of-a-Kind Family*, there was no wrangling over what values were important, and no time spent in fear of passing on wrong values. The prescription was clear, and the path illuminated. For thousands of years, Jewish families kept the same feasts, read the same Torah, and passed on the same heritage. Each year during the fall feasts of Rosh Hashanah and Yom Kippur, they would take time as a family to repent of the ways they had strayed from the path and commit themselves to do better in the coming year. The Jewish culture stayed strong despite persecution because of the anchors of celebration and ritual. The antidote to the fear of children leaving the faith, or living in opposition to their values, was a hearty effort toward passing on not only a set of rules, but a whole culture.

The weekly Sabbath was part of these anchors. In *All-of-a-Kind Family*, Mama prepares for the Sabbath with the rush of cleaning and cooking that precedes any holiday. Then, as the Friday sun sinks into the horizon, the family welcomes the day of rest and reflection, the weekly ritual that set them apart from many modern families. The welcoming of the ritual is described in words that make me long for this in my own family.

> The children stood around the table watching her. A lovely feeling of peace and contentment seemed to flow out from Mama to them. First, she put a napkin on her head; then placing four white candles in the brass candlesticks, she lit them. . . . After that Mama covered her eyes with her hands, softly murmuring a prayer in Hebrew.
> Thus was the Sabbath ushered in.[1]

But celebrating a day of rest isn't a ritual God commands just so that our bodies and minds are ready for another day of work. And I don't think that God asks us to rest just so we can lose a day of work, either. In his book *The Sabbath*, Jewish rabbi Abraham Joshua Heschel describes the Sabbath as an invitation: "Observance of the seventh day is more than a technique of fulfilling a commandment. The Sabbath is the presence of God in the world, open to the soul of man. It is possible for the soul to respond in affection, to enter into fellowship with the consecrated day."[2]

Heschel's description of the Sabbath makes me think that God wanted more than just a rest day for us. He wanted a rest day *with* us. He wanted a day set apart when we would be with him, and whether we realize it or not—whether the Jewish family who is keeping the Sabbath is aware of God's presence or not—God promises to bless those who honor the keeping of this special day.

The passing down of rituals, the values driving them made clear, can help our children carry on the values of their parents, and if one of those rituals is keeping the Sabbath, here is the promise from God for those who honor this day: "Then you shall take delight in the LORD, and I will make you ride on the heights of the earth; I will feed you with the heritage of Jacob your father" (Isaiah 58:14).

For many of us, taking a day to rest seems impossible, but I think what is lost when we don't pause in our week to connect with each other and with God is too precious to neglect. My husband and I went on a tour of Israel a few years ago, and we happened to be there during a holy day. It struck me deeply how these families observed the day together. We visited some of the sites around Jerusalem, the brook where David picked up a stone to fight Goliath, and the oasis where Rebekah was watering the animals when Isaac's servant found her. After a few stunning hours we stopped in a hotel for a lunch break, and we noticed families sitting in large groups in the lobby. With the remains of lunch still scattered about, they sat together visiting and enjoying each other, children and adults in the same group. Out on the patio a woman was in a chair reading a book. Nearby, an older man was taking a nap. They were resting in a way that I don't see in America.

So often when we see people on holiday, they are separate, the teens slumped over their phones while adults talk, and younger children run between them. It's rare to see families sitting together, screen-free, just talking, but it gave me vision to continue to fight for time like that with my own children, to fight for rest days and family days, and time to just enjoy each other's presence and the presence of God. I think that as we carve out these weekly anchors, we are giving our children something to hang on to. We can't guarantee an outcome for them, and no matter how much ritual we build in, we still must face down fear and release our children to God. However, when we observe days to rest and experience the presence of God, we are inviting our children into a relationship. Ritual may eventually grow cold, but if the ritual leads to a relationship, if it leads us to know the Lover of our souls, then we can know we aren't just releasing our children to God, we are releasing them to friendship with God.

Another way *All-of-a-Kind Family* helped me fight fear was in seeing how much fun they had together. Even going to the synagogue carried a sense of fun: "Armed with rattle wheels and horns, Papa and the children left the house. They were a merry group, with the five little girls dancing circles around Papa all the way. It was wonderful to be young today. Nobody cared how much noise they made. . . . Friends and relatives showered them with happy Purim greetings; even strangers hailed them as they passed on the streets."[3]

I had read this description of their joy, but it was stunning to actually witness it when my husband and I were in Jerusalem during a holy day. The narrow streets of the city were packed tightly with families hurrying toward the Western Wall. Tiny girls in dresses and little boys in suits hurried along with their mothers and fathers to reach the wall, where they would pray in the same spot where their ancestors had prayed for thousands of years. They were rushing toward the wall, singing and shouting as they went, the excitement pulsating through the air. As we came into the square where thousands were pressed close to the wall, swaying as they prayed, I stood above observing for a few minutes. Nearby sat a Jewish woman with one child on her lap and several more nearby. I asked her how they continue to pass on their faith and values to their children, and she said, "We try to make it fun." She told me that while they are communicating their values to their children, they do it with a spirit of joy and laughter—it's an invitation instead of a prison sentence.

In our own family, we intentionally cultivated joyful traditions and closeness through our recreation. We took thrilling raft rides through treacherous canyons and summer camping trips to the beach. We celebrated fall with backyard weenie roasts and trips to the apple orchard for fresh apple cider donuts and crisp apples. Winter was spent sledding down a nearby hill, reading by the fire, and baking together. And spring was marked by our observance of the Passover, with the heartfelt rituals of unleavened bread and wine, and the four questions centering our celebrations in the redemption won by the precious Lamb of God.

In *All-of-a-Kind Family*, so many of the family values were part of their festivals as well. The teaching about how to stay close to God was folded into a feast, and everybody loves a feast. As they celebrated Passover, they were reminded of God's deliverance and encouraged to give him thanks, followed by a game of hide-and-seek with the unleavened bread. As they celebrated Rosh Hashanah, they threw breadcrumbs in the water to symbolize our sins being removed from us "as far as the east is from the west" (even after thousands of years, children still love throwing things in water). As they celebrated Succoth, they built an outdoor structure and decorated it with fragrant greenery to remember how God protected them in the desert. Every holiday has a built-in memorial to God's faithfulness with built-in fun. How can the Jewish people forget God when they are constantly reminded in these joyful ways? How can they walk away when the sweetness of every celebration is enfolded in the stories of God's goodness to them?

This doesn't mean we all have to start keeping the Jewish feasts in order to keep our children, but it should make us think about how we have fun. In Deuteronomy 6, God is impressing on his people the importance of passing on his laws. "And these words that I command you today shall be on your heart. You shall teach them diligently to your children, and shall talk of them when you sit in your house, and when you walk by the way, and when you lie down, and when you rise" (Deuteronomy 6:6–7).

In the Jewish culture, much of the fun and celebration is tied together with passing on the faith, but for many Christians, our lives tend to be compartmentalized. Church is on Sunday, while Bible teaching is often not even done by the parents, but instead is outsourced to a teacher, and the fun we have is separate from our faith. Our children begin to equate faith with Sunday mornings, and fun is everything else. When we start to incorporate the values we want to pass on to our children into everyday life, we begin to see them make an impact. We see our children develop their own love for God, based on the opportunities we've created for them to make that connection. So if you are struggling to start some traditions, here are a few suggestions.

1. **Start having a special weekly meal.** Set the table, light some candles, and speak a blessing over your children (chapter 4 on speaking life has some suggestions for wording).

2. **Incorporate your faith into your celebrations.** Read the Christmas story before you open presents, or act out the resurrection before you hunt for eggs. Start celebrating a Reformation night or a saints night once a year, dressing up as a hero of the faith and eating

special food to commemorate the evening. Try celebrating the Jewish feasts; as Christians, we are grafted into the family of Abraham, and celebrating Jewish feasts is an opportunity to experience God more deeply.

3. **Begin daily traditions of reading the Bible together.** It could be read at the dinner table when you are all seated together, or it could be a bedtime ritual. You could read from a favorite devotional or just read the psalm that corresponds with the date, but making family memories around Scripture is a powerful way to anchor your children and to fight fear.

4. **Start service traditions with your children.** There's nothing quite as fun as taking a family mission trip or delivering pizza to a homeless camp. You could knit baby hats for a shelter or shop for food and give it to a food pantry together. Putting faith into action with your children will make a huge impact.

5. **Start spending regular time in nature together.** Playing in the water, taking walks among tall trees, and looking for bugs under rocks are all delightful ways of connecting with your children and connecting them to God.

As you create a family culture and traditions around your values and make them happy ones, you are inviting your children into your own delight in God and letting go of fear. In America, we may have to work harder to have a strong family culture because we are such a melting pot, but it's worth the effort. Despite the many different cultures Americans come from, the schools have become the culture for kids, and immigrant parents are shamed into going along with it. My own great-grandparents, fresh off the boat from Hungary, didn't pass on the language to their children, and many of the immigrants throughout the 1900s were similarly pressured to abandon their culture of origin and conform to American values. They were afraid that their kids would be outcasts. They wanted their kids to fit in, to be "all-American," and in the process, started losing the values and traditions that made their family culture. We've been taught to be more afraid of being different than of raising our own children, to the detriment of our culture and the world at large. Psychologist Leonard Sax writes in *The Collapse of Parenting*, "Part of your job as parents is to educate desire. To teach your child to go beyond, 'whatever floats your boat.' To enjoy, and to want to enjoy, pleasures higher and deeper than video games and social media can provide. Those pleasures may be found perhaps in conversation with wise adults, or in meditation, prayer, or reflection; or in music, dance, or the arts. The parent-child attachment has to be the first priority."[4]

So while we need to push back on fear, we can take the time to educate desire instead of throwing wide open the doorway to leave the faith. When most of our children's lives are secular, and God is just something we tack on to Sunday mornings, a requisite church visit in the midst of an otherwise God-empty life, I think the fear is grounded in some reality. In a study done by Lifeway Research, 66 percent of college students stop going to church after attending regularly in the teen years.[5] Their lives become increasingly full, and God has no place in the busyness. But when we adopt a lifestyle that celebrates God in nature, in our holidays, even in our daily lives, our children can't help but love him too.

My parents might have been wounded by church and lost their Christian community for a while, but the example they set of faithfulness and of daily seeking God was noted by their children. All five of us love Jesus. All five of us have given our children a Christian education, whether at home or in a private school setting. And all five of us continue to create a culture that reflects our faith in our homes.

> When we adopt a lifestyle that celebrates God in nature, in our holidays, even in our daily lives, our children can't help but love him too.

Even if you haven't yet invited your children into your faith and values, even if fear has kept you from making a move or taken the joy out of it, it's never too late to start. It's never too late to help your children "taste and see that the LORD is good; Blessed is the man who trusts in Him!" (Psalm 34:8 NKJV). It's never too late to create a culture of joy and start traditions that become anchors for the souls of your children.

CHAPTER SIX
Study Guide

In what ways did your parents pass on their values?

What family traditions did you grow up with?

What family traditions will you start with?

Download the free family vision guide from the Peaceful Press at https://www.thepeacefulpreschool.com/blog/creating-a-family-vision.

A VERSE TO MEMORIZE

And these words that I command you today shall be on your heart. You shall teach them diligently to your children, and shall talk of them when you sit in your house, and when you walk by the way, and when you lie down, and when you rise.

DEUTERONOMY 6:6–7

MORE BOOKS ON
Family Traditions

To Read Aloud
Beni's Family Treasury: Stories for the Jewish Holidays by Jane Breskin Zalben
The Chosen by Chaim Potok
A Papa Like Everyone Else by Sydney Taylor

For Mom
Garden City by John Mark Comer
The Sabbath by Abraham Joshua Heschel

Overcome the Fear of Failing Our Children by Living for a Greater Purpose

We've got to play at being poor for a bit.

E. Nesbit, *The Railway Children*

On the long drive home from a weekend at Lord's Land, my husband and I talked and dreamed about our future while our three young children slept soundly in the back seat. We had been taking trips to YWAM's rustic coastal retreat center since our oldest was an infant, and the rough wood cabins with Scripture verses marking the path to the woods and the walking trails hemmed with ferns and moss in the quiet, ancient forest enchanted us. Each visit fueled the dream of living simply and close to nature. The desire to live a quiet country life with a flock of chickens in the backyard and fragrant lilacs growing by the front porch was crystallizing into action steps to pursue this dream.

As my husband drove the sunny California roads back home to our suburban house, we wrote down those action steps and the values guiding us toward this simple life we dreamed of. We wanted to live a quiet life, to work with our hands. We wanted to be involved in missions, to show hospitality, and we wanted our lives to be a testimony to the Lover of our souls, Jesus.

We wrote down identity statements for our children as well, based on what we could already see in them or what we hoped to see. Instead of labeling them with curses ("he's so clingy," "she's so bossy"), we called them out as leaders, worshipers, and artisans, even though they were just five, three, and one. We called out the gifts we believed were in them and envisioned children who would love others well, who would be skilled at playing instruments, who would care about the poor.

We had a purpose greater than ourselves, and we pursued that purpose as a family. We read books about gardening and missionaries; we cultivated a life focused on loving God and loving others. Because we had a vision for it and weren't distracted by a million other pursuits, we were able to purchase a small home in the country, get music lessons for our children, plant a garden, and start taking mission trips.

But with the realization of some of these dreams came more significant challenges. Our adventure as missionaries in Mexico, while being the culmination of a dream, also served to kill our dreams and burn up much of our innocence and excitement. It was much harder than anticipated, and the subsequent fighting between my husband and me left us with a feeling of failure, of being far from the model family we aspired to be. It also killed much of our missionary zeal as we assessed the high level of stress it initiated because of the health issues our children had faced and the challenges of living in a foreign country. When we finally moved back to California after four taxing years, we were weary and adrift, our vision cloudy and faltering.

Upon our return, my husband focused on providing for the seven children we now had, often working out of town, and I felt alone in the struggle to raise my children for Christ. We no longer had a missionary adventure to look forward to; we had to move to a new area for work, and so much was out of our control as we entered the teen years with our children. It's easy to hold on to vision when it feels like you have some autonomy over your life, but when circumstances seem to thwart your ability to choose, fear comes in. I wanted my children to love Jesus and live purposefully; I wanted them to pursue good works and love the Word, to "walk in a manner worthy of the calling" to which they were called.[1] But in this season, I felt no support from my husband and was muddling along by myself.

As I was struggling through this lonely time, I read *The Railway Children* by Edith Nesbit. The Waterburys were a perfectly happy family, with a father who was never cross, and with a mother who wrote poetry for their birthdays and read aloud to them. They lived in a home in London with every modern convenience, until one day when their father was mysteriously taken away. Suddenly their lives changed drastically, and they had to live on a rough country road in a little house where rats could be heard scampering in the walls. Mother tried to make it a game;

"We've got to play at being poor for a bit," she said as they left behind their beautiful home and belongings for an unknown future.[2]

It reminded me of our own story. We had worked so hard to create a dream life for our children, and we were such a happy family, so full of purpose, before we went on our missionary adventure. Sadly, our lack of skills in working through conflict left us demoralized upon our return, and we had lost our vision. But as I read about how Mother in *The Railway Children* lived according to her lights, lived into purpose despite their difficult circumstances, I was lifted, and strength returned for the journey. You see, Mother wasn't sitting there wringing her hands and blaming her husband's absence for her lack of action. She didn't throw in the towel on doing good because she was doing it alone.

> As I read about how Mother in The Railway Children lived into purpose despite their difficult circumstances, I was lifted, and strength returned for the journey.

I think we often deal with the fear that because our husband isn't on board with our vision or isn't supportive, it's going to fail, and we just give up altogether. We underestimate the power to inspire that we have as women and as mothers, and we give in to fear instead of living by faith. Living with a purpose, living with a clear vision of what you are working toward, is a powerful antidote to fear. "Where there is no vision, the people perish" (Proverbs 29:18 KJV), and it feels like we are perishing when we try to meet too many expectations and struggle along with no clear idea of where we are going.

We are afraid that our kids will fall behind, worried that we are failing them and fearful that they won't be good people. And in our fear, it's easy to start blaming our husbands for their lack of initiative in helping us and inspiring our children. And sadly, we often stay so busy trying to do everything and blaming others for our issues that we don't even make time to figure out what our vision might be. But what is it that keeps us mindlessly busy and makes it hard for us to create space to think and plan? What makes it hard for us to say no to activities and say yes to living for a higher calling?

What is it that prohibits us from finding and following a vision?

The culture we live in might be partly to blame. We are constantly faced with new choices and marketing campaigns designed to make us feel less-than unless we buy the advertised product. Greg McKeown writes in his book *Essentialism*, "What if society stopped telling us to buy more stuff and instead allowed us to create more space to breathe and think? What if society encouraged us to reject what has been accurately described as doing things we detest, to buy things we don't need, with money we don't have, to impress people we don't like?"[3]

Most people's lives are defined by subtle and not-so-subtle lessons learned from society. Lessons such as *having cool stuff makes us cool*. In order to have cool stuff, we need to have a good job, and life is mostly about earning money and buying cool stuff; therefore, we need to get a good education so we can get a good job so we can buy cool stuff. British educator Charlotte Mason writes, "The educational thought we hear most about is, as I have said, based on sundry Darwinian axioms, out of which we get the notion that nothing matters but physical fitness and vocational training. However important these are, they are not the chief thing. . . . The period when Germany made her school curriculum utilitarian marks the beginning of her moral downfall."[4]

Charlotte was pointing out, nearly a hundred years ago, that this focus on simply getting skills that lead to a good job was contributing to moral decline and ultimately being out of touch with our own spiritual life and the spiritual health of our world. If it was true then, it's frighteningly accurate now. But we don't have to live a utilitarian life focused solely on impressing people. We can live for a higher purpose. Even in those seasons when we are paving the way alone, even when we are afraid, we can live for love.

In *The Railway Children*, the family suffered a reversal of fortune, leaving behind their comfortable London life for a tenuous existence by the railroad tracks. They were without the comforting presence of their father and were struggling alone, not knowing if he would ever be back. They didn't allow these setbacks to change who they were. This family didn't allow setbacks to keep them from loving others, from serving those in need, or from living for a higher purpose. Their vision and identity didn't change just because their circumstances did. Mother didn't wait for her husband to be home to do the next right thing. She just did what was in front of her to do.

But society can be very distracting, and it's a hard push to keep vision alive and overcome fear when surrounded by advertising meant to distract us. I love *The Lego Movie* and its commentary on our society. In the beginning, just as Emmet, the protagonist, begins to gain some awareness of what is really happening around him, he hears an evil sound bite from the president, but as soon as he starts to wonder about it, a fast-paced show comes on that distracts him. A catchy tune prevents Emmet from asking serious questions about why Lord Business intends to use the Kragle to freeze them all on Taco Tuesday. Emmet is distracted from the evil plan against them by slick advertising and mind-numbing jingles.

We can make some parallels here. How many of us set aside time to think about what we are doing as a family and why? It is easy to get busy with life and just keep saying yes to whatever opportunity is presented, with no real forethought about what the cost is to our family. Rabbi Abraham Heschel writes in *The Sabbath*, "In spite of our triumphs we have fallen victim to the work of our hands. It is as if the forces we have conquered have conquered us."[5]

So the first step to overcoming fear in order to live with vision—the first step to getting off the hamster wheel and out of the rat race—is to take some time to evaluate our lives and what actually matters. I would like to propose that what really matters is *people*, and especially loving the people God has put in our sphere of influence. Greg McKeown writes, "What if we stopped celebrating being busy as a measurement of importance? What if instead we celebrated how much time we had spent listening, pondering, meditating, and enjoying time with the most important people in our lives?"[6]

But loving people well requires a certain amount of self-awareness. John Calvin writes, "Without knowledge of self there is no knowledge of God."[7] God has made each of us with unique gifts and unique callings. The things I love are not necessarily what some of you will love, but *what* we love is a clue to *how* we can love well, and ultimately how we can live with vision, even in those seasons when we are afraid and alone.

In *The Railway Children*, Mother was the same person even when her circumstances changed. She didn't blame her husband for the situation, and neither did she give up on her higher purpose because her life was different. She was consistent with what was important to her, grounded even, so she was able to reject fear. She kept writing her stories and loving her children, trusting that God, who began a good work, would be faithful to complete it.[8] She trusted that all would be well again, even when she could see no reason to believe so.

Maybe knowing who we are is a good start to overcoming fear. Perhaps instead of blaming our husbands for their lack of vision and direction, we should ask ourselves, *What are we living for? What makes us come alive? What makes us feel excited and hopeful?* Think back to the last time you really enjoyed yourself and remember what it was you were doing. Instead of waiting for our husbands to get excited about life and provide vision for our children, we can stop blaming and living in fear and start getting clear about our own vision and purpose. We can just move forward with our loving and serving, despite the lack of support. We don't have to give up on life just because those around us have.

French hero Joan of Arc kept living for a bigger purpose, kept listening to the still, small voice of God, even when she was abandoned by family and friends, misunderstood, and maligned. She didn't let fear rule her life, she lived for a higher purpose, and she led her people into freedom, and as I began to shake off fear, I found fresh vision for my life and family as well. I didn't wait for everything to be perfect to start learning how to garden, or write, or teach my children. I started getting excited about the future and in the process overcame debilitating fear.

But how do we translate ideals into action? How do we develop a vision and move forward with it instead of waiting, paralyzed, for something to change? Here are three steps to get started.

1. **Write It Down.** I begin by writing down what I love and what my loved ones love. I pay attention to what makes us come alive, and I make a note of it. I don't live for what everyone around me is doing; instead, I notice what we have been created to do.

2. **Order Your Days.** Once I've taken time to brainstorm and write down what we love and what makes us come alive, I take time to see whether our vision and calling is in sync with my life. I look at my schedule and what my children are involved in and evaluate whether it reflects our values and vision or if we are spending our time on pursuits that are meaningless to us.

   For me, this is a continual process of evaluating my daily and weekly activities. My vision of putting people above things can often get crowded out by caring for the things that I buy those people and the activities that I involve us in.

3. **Keep the Vision in Sight.** In the early days of our marriage, on that memorable trip home from Lord's Land, we had written down what we loved as a family, and the activities we had listed were based on what we already loved doing. We tended to spend our free time outside, and both my husband and I had an interest in missionary work in foreign countries. Traveling and working with people in other cultures made us come alive. There were clues early on that

being outside, helping people, and travel were our loves; these were the life goals that we would work toward.

Having defined this early on, in a time when we weren't wounded and weary, helped me to know what to keep doing in a season when my husband was unable to dream with me. I believe this is what helped Mother in *The Railway Children* as well. They were already a strong family, active in helping others and nurturing their children, so when a temporary setback came along, they just kept living into their purpose.

The ironic thing about living with vision is that a side effect of pursuing something greater than yourself, of living with purpose, can be the weariness and death of vision that comes when we face the eventual back draft. The Israelites followed the vision God gave them to leave Egypt and then hit weariness as they wandered in the desert. Paul the apostle followed God's call to preach the gospel and faced imprisonment and torture, and Hebrews 11 is a poetic example of the backlash faced when, by faith, the people of God followed his leading. You can read any missionary biography, or the stories of inventors and artists, to see this same pattern. Overcoming the fear of man to live into a higher purpose will create opportunities to overcome more fear as we face the obstacles inherent in a meaningful life. N. D. Wilson in *Death by Living* writes, "The truth is that a life well lived is always lived on a rising scale of difficulty."[9]

Often when we step out in faith in pursuit of a vision, there is a free fall, this period of testing before you find your groove. It's like childbirth: We get this vision of having a child and then proceed toward pregnancy, but along the way, there is a period when we've been puking up our guts for a few months when we might ask ourselves, *What have I done?* If any of you have gone through natural childbirth, you know that there is also a period during labor when you just want to shut it down and go back to being pregnant. Even knowing that there is a beautiful little baby to hold on the other side is often not enough to prevent that feeling, the desperation to crawl off the birthing table and keep that baby inside, to do anything to shut down the pain and escape the ring of fire that is transition and birth.

Living with vision is like that. You take the time to evaluate who you are and what you love. You start to prepare for the vision, and then a door opens, but often there is a ring of fire to pass through before we get to the promised land, that next area of influence or purpose God has for us. But Robert Frost writes about hardship: "The best way out is always through."[10]

The best way out of a homeschool day that's gone bad is just to sit down on the couch and read some books together until bedtime. The best way out of that season of sleepless nights is to just keep thanking God for babies and catching sleep where you can. We don't quit the vision—we push through to the other side, even when we are afraid or alone.

We've been through that ring of fire many times. My husband had a vision for mission work in Mexico. It was good and holy work, but it flattened us for several years afterward. Our family then found some healing and new vision that preceded our going on a fantastic mission trip to Tanzania, where we led a group of missionaries through a marriage class we facilitated. It was a beautiful time of preparation for us, and it birthed a new vision of having a paid-for home so we could have more resources to devote to our vision and more time to devote to people. We prayed through the idea of selling our house and downsizing, and as a family we felt that this was how God was leading. As I prayed, I could picture a cute house near a creek, a house pretty enough that I was willing to sell my beautiful five-acre farm, with its prolific fruit trees, fertile gardens, tree forts and ponds, and a deep pool for swimming.

We went through the sale process in faith, trusting that God would provide the house we had asked for. The journey, however, was about a thousand times harder than I expected it would be. We couldn't close on a house while we were in the sale process, and we ended up having to rent a tiny one-bathroom house, far from town and devoid of yard space or internet. A house that, while we were in the sale process, I had petulantly said I would never live in. We lived there for three months, and there were a few moments when I was tempted to think God was punishing me for hiding in the bathroom checking Instagram too often in my last house, because being in a one-bathroom house with nine people meant that bathroom time was limited and precious.

Then, the only house we could find to purchase within our budget was a major fixer-upper that required ripping it down to the studs to get a floor plan we could live with. The whole process was so difficult, and so off the mark of my vision of gaining more time as a family and more resources for missions. But this process was very different from our time in Mexico because of some lessons we had learned. Trying to back out of the difficulties while we were in Mexico, constantly complaining, feeling sorry for myself and my children, and eventually falling into depression and marital discord had caused the time of testing—the wandering in the desert—to be prolonged and devastatingly painful. I was constantly looking back, in the process stagnating our family vision and ultimately causing pain to my children, which was exactly what I had hoped to protect them from.

But I had learned my lesson, and so this time, when we were faced with camping out on the property, cooking outside in 100-degree heat while dealing with contractors, and starting my first days of homeschool in a stifling little travel trailer instead of a beautiful schoolroom, I rode it out cheerfully. When my husband and I couldn't agree on the placement of the kitchen sink, and our communication broke down over petty decisions, I kept forgiving and hoping for happier days. I kept cheerfully navigating the difficulties, cooking meals for my family in an Instant Pot and rice cooker for months while waiting for the kitchen remodel, washing dishes on the back patio, and sleeping in the yard as windows were installed and the floors refinished. We turned the whole experience into a game, even hosting house guests during the remodel, and made what might have been a terrible trial into a happy memory. I finally understood that trials don't hurt our children; it's our attitude about the trials that hurts them. When we can cheerfully overcome our fear and face the storms, even self-inflicted storms from choosing a different path, we teach our children far more about navigating life than if we had just stayed safely on the shore, living without vision.

The Railway Children was an inspiration during this time of testing. The way Mother kept cheerfully doing the next thing—loving others and caring for her family despite the absence of her husband—helped me to keep loving and serving, keep doing the next thing even when our vision was cloudy or when my husband was discouraged and we weren't on the same page.

So what brought about this change for me, this new ability to be cheerful even when I was afraid? I truly believe that forgiveness is the key. I'll dive deeper into the process of forgiveness in a later chapter, but when we live with bitterness about how we have been treated, even bitterness toward ourselves about how we have treated others, we shut down our awareness of how loved we are, and fear comes in. Fear is the belief that we are alone in the world, that nobody is watching out for us. Fear is the opposite of trust.

Once I took the time to thoroughly forgive my parents, my husband, and myself for the pain I had experienced as a child, and for the pain I had experienced in our first brave attempt as a couple to live with vision, I was able to follow our new vision from a place of knowing I was loved. In my first big experience of stepping out in faith, I had looked at my life through the lens of a victim. I had complained about my life, suspecting that nobody loved me, not even God. This caused me to look at every experience as a personal attack.

Once I had forgiven myself and others, I began to live from a different place. My eyes were opened to how truly loved I was by God, and this gave me the ability to evaluate each trial differently. Now, instead of assuming that a difficult experience was God punishing me for something, I experienced events as an opportunity to grow. In *Ruthless Trust* Brennan Manning writes about our experience of love, "The splendor of a human heart which trusts it is loved gives God more

> Once I had forgiven myself and others, my eyes were opened to how truly loved I was by God, and this gave me the ability to evaluate each trial differently.

pleasure than Westminster Cathedral, the Sistine Chapel, Beethoven's Ninth Symphony, Van Gogh's *Sunflowers*, the sight of ten thousand butterflies in flight, or the scent of a million orchids in bloom. Trust is our gift back to God, and he finds it so enchanting that Jesus died for love of it."[11]

When we know we are loved unconditionally, we can trust and be bold to follow a different path, to be a spectacle, to do something that is brave—something as simple as choosing to homeschool our children or to buy a smaller house so we have more money for a higher purpose, or choosing to spend more time on art than on math, or on math than on reading. We can clear our schedules of nonessentials and bravely invest ourselves into relationships. Medieval mystic Lady Julian of Norwich is credited with writing this prayer: "Lord, let not our souls be busy inns that have no room for thee or thine, but quiet homes of prayer and praise, where thou mayest find fit company, where the needful cares of life are wisely ordered and put away, and wide, sweet spaces kept for thee; where holy thoughts pass up and down and fervent longings watch and wait thy coming."[12]

When we know we are loved passionately and audaciously by God, when we have forgiven others, especially our own dear husbands, and opened the gates to experiencing God's love, we can live with childlike faith. We can return to joy and hope for the future. Children bravely try new things and follow the spark. They dance on dewy grass in bare feet, and laugh over bright balloons, and are comfortable in their own skin. We can get back to that place too, that place of fearlessness, of dreaming big, of believing that you could be anything. We can get back to that place of knowing that our big Daddy in heaven is watching out for us, and as all the best of childhood is renewed in us, we can save childhood for our own dear children.

CHAPTER SEVEN
Study Guide

Write down three things your family loves to do.

Review the family vision guide you downloaded from the Peaceful Press at https://www.thepeacefulpreschool.com /blog/creating-a-family-vision and filled out after chapter 6.

What aspects of your vision can you keep following even when your spouse is unsupportive or discouraged?

Is there someone you need to forgive so you can open the way to trust again?

A VERSE TO MEMORIZE

There is no fear in love, but perfect love casts out fear.

1 JOHN 4:18

MORE BOOKS ABOUT

Living for a Greater Purpose

To Read Aloud

Mary Emma & Company by Ralph Moody

Swallows and Amazons by Arthur Ransome

For Mom

Ruthless Trust by Brennan Manning

The Prize Winner of Defiance, Ohio by Terry Ryan

Overcome the Fear of the Future by Not Complaining

If wisdom's ways you wisely seek,
Five things observe with care,
To whom you speak,
Of whom you speak,
and how and when and where.

Laura Ingalls Wilder,
Little Town on the Prairie

Our missionary adventure in Mexico began right after my fifth child turned two. The day we arrived was drizzly and cold, and muddy footprints were tracked through our rental as the maintenance team tried to find a propane leak. The house smelled of propane, that slightly poopy smell reminiscent of rotten eggs that companies add so we are not killed by undetected natural gas leaks. We had left behind our beloved country home nearly a month prior, the renters moving in as we were moving out. And while I was thankful to have my family in our own home again (we'd lived for a month in my sister's one-room pool house), this place scared me. The house was a tiny two-story condo in a Baja beach community, with one upstairs bedroom containing a double bed, and another bedroom with several twin beds on the ground floor near the exit. All five of our children were squeezed into that room, the toddler sleeping in a playpen while the other four each had a twin bed. The idea of my precious children sleeping on the ground floor so near to the door was terrifying to me. We had already heard stories of the rise in kidnapping cases in Baja, so we were trying to wedge wood into the sliding door so it couldn't be opened, and I was trying to soothe my own fears.

I wanted to muster up the courage to make this move fun for my kids, but I was awash with terror about our new life. As a young mother of five children, I worried about their health, their safety, and how we could continue to be a happy family under the intense circumstances of missionary life. I had read so many missionary biographies, and while stories so often have empowered me to be brave, many of those missionary stories had involved losing children to disease, or worse. There was the story of John and Betty Stam, who were killed in China during the Boxer Rebellion, while their infant miraculously survived alone in the house until she was rescued by fellow missionaries. Then there was the story of Jonathan and Rosalind Goforth, Presbyterian missionaries in China who had experienced the joy and power of the Holy

Spirit, but not until they had lost five of their eleven children to sickness. I wanted to be a good missionary for Jesus, but I also wanted to give my children a happy childhood, and I was afraid that I couldn't do both.

Honestly, I was afraid of a lot more than that. I was afraid my children would get sick. I was afraid they would be kidnapped. I was afraid they would feel deprived, and I was afraid that my own fears would make them fearful. A mess of swirling fears caused me to freeze up and ultimately stole my joy. We had been such a happy family in our old life. I had created a magical life for my children in that quiet canyon with the rocky creek running through it. I hosted springtime picnics, my friends and I sipping coffee while our children hunted chocolate eggs, held gunnysack races in the field, and looked for tadpoles in the creek. After church on Sundays, we would take our canoe up the mountain to a granite-bottom lake, the older children cooling off in the clear blue water while our toddler stood at attention in the prow of the boat, scanning the horizon like a good little seaman. I missed that life, and I was afraid that we were shortchanging them in our new life. Many of my fears proved to be unfounded, but the fear opened a door for conflict in my marriage as my worrying caused me to shut down and look at the dark side of every situation.

As I went through this difficult season, I was reading aloud the whole LITTLE HOUSE ON THE PRAIRIE series by Laura Ingalls Wilder. I read *Little House on the Prairie*, about their long trip across the empty prairie, while we were taking our own long trip down the interstate in the middle of winter. I read *On the Banks of Plum Creek*, about the family settling into a new community, while we were trying to find new friends in our south-of-the-border community, and I read *By the Shores of Silver Lake*, about the Ingalls family spending a lonely winter at a surveyor's cabin, while we were spending our own lonely Christmas in Mexico. And we read *The Long Winter*, that saga of the winter when the trains couldn't come through and the Ingalls family nearly starved, as we were experiencing our own long January, living off the power grid and often stranded at home because of the slick roads during a rainstorm. While reading the history of Laura's pioneer life aloud to my children, I pioneered through my own life, overcame my tendency to complain, and became a braver mom. I watched how Ma faced down her own fears, and it gave me strength to overcome my wild imagination and gave hope to my terrified heart.

Our Imagination Can Be Used against Us

Perhaps you can relate to my vivid imagination when it comes to fear? I read Scarlet Hiltibidal's *Afraid of All the Things* and realized that I was not alone in conjuring up fearsome situations seemingly out of thin air. It seems to be something we mothers are especially proficient at, and I imagine that you have the same anxiety-producing skill. Hiltibidal writes, "Those early days of motherhood were some of the most terrifying of my life. I wasn't afraid of being a bad mom. I was afraid of absurd things. I was afraid of other people holding her and not being gentle enough. I was afraid of getting carjacked and watching a black-market baby seller drive off with her every time I left the house."[1]

Many of us have the same ability to imagine absurd worst-case scenarios. We buy our kids a trampoline and then cringe in terror, imagining that they will fall off and concuss themselves on a rock. We take a nature walk and a scene starts playing in our head of our child being bitten by a snake as she runs through the brush. Somebody coughs in our presence and we instantly start planning for how we will survive a bout of pneumonia. We've cultivated the ability to imagine, even to feel, the terror of worst-case scenarios, which only reveals how far we are from our Father. While we confess Christianity with our mouths, we are more influenced by the bad news of the world than by the Word of God.

Complaint-Filled Communication Corrupts Joy

I think the secret to Pa and Ma making it through so many truly horrific experiences was their commitment to not give way to their emotions, the steely resolve to take their thoughts captive instead of being enslaved by them. Ma displays this resolve in her words and actions time and time again. Her words "least said, soonest mended"[2] reminded me of the biblical instruction to "let no corrupting talk come out of your mouths, but only such as is good for building up, as fits the occasion, that it may give grace to those who hear" (Ephesians 4:29). It's a verse I've repeated often to my children in an effort to get them to speak kindly to each other, or to not complain to me, but I was sadly unaware of how my own complaint-filled communication was corrupting my joy and creating fear.

When we left behind our beautiful little farm in the canyon and started our adventure in Mexico, I gave myself permission to complain about my life, to focus on all that

> I think the secret to Pa and Ma Ingalls making it through so many horrific experiences was their commitment to not give way to their emotions, to take their thoughts captive.

was wrong with it, and then to assume that because I had some trials in my life, God hated me. Instead of focusing on all that was right in my life, I let my mind dwell on what was out of order. I let fear take the lead, and it was taking me down a path to destruction, a path of dissatisfaction and despair.

Feeling discontented seemed so innocent too. I felt I had a right to air my grievances about my current life. I had given up tall trees, my quiet valley, our beautiful new SUV, community, family, financial security, and my beloved mountain creeks and lakes, and I felt I had the right to at least complain a little about what we had left behind. I felt that my unhappiness was justified, and I made no effort to find the beauty in my new life. But God has a direct command to not complain, with clear reasons given: "Do all things without grumbling or disputing, that you may be blameless and innocent, children of God without blemish in the midst of a crooked and twisted generation, among whom you shine as lights in the world" (Philippians 2:14–15).

Complaining causes harm. It diminishes our light, and it was certainly dimming my light as a mother. The more I complained, the more I slid into depression, and this depression was stealing my enjoyment of my children. I was so fearful about robbing them of a happy childhood, but all that was needed for a happy childhood for them was a happy mother. When Ma Ingalls was struggling to recover after the long winter and the decimation of much-needed crops by hungry blackbirds, this sums up her attitude: "'This earthly life is a battle,' said Ma. 'If it isn't one thing to contend with, it's another. It always has been so, and it always will be. The sooner you make up your mind to that, the better off you are, and the more thankful for your pleasures.'"[3]

She said this when she had actual hardships to complain about. She said it and still managed to be joyful when her children were in actual danger of going hungry. My own situation, the one where I was complaining and letting my focus on the dark side of life lead me into depression, was much, much different. We were missionaries in Tijuana, Mexico. It was far from home and family, a different culture and language, and we weren't on our pretty property in the country anymore. I could find plenty to complain about, but the truth of the matter is that there was also great beauty in my life.

I was on an adventure with my family, and my husband was home every day. We were living near the beach and were learning a new language. We had money in the bank after the sale of a business and money coming in from the renting of our home. We were in no danger of going hungry, and we had an amazing opportunity to experience this adventure together. I weep now as I think of how I squandered that season with my complaining. To many people, our life was a dream, and we were a dream family, but I wasted the joy of that season and opened the door to fear with my lack of self-control over my thoughts and words. If I would have just taken Ma Ingalls's advice and recognized that in this life there will be trouble, I could have enjoyed that season. I could have embraced the blessings and slammed the door on fear. Instead of being a season that opened the door to destruction in our family, it could have been the best time of our lives.

Maybe you are in a similar situation. Life isn't what you hoped it would be, and you are daily surprised by how hard it is. Your expectations are dashed. Maybe you thought parenting a toddler was going to be a magical experience full of Instagram-worthy moments, and you now realize that it mostly consists of setting the timer so they don't pee on the floor. Maybe you imagined that having a family was going to be easier, more fun, like a #childhoodunplugged photo with cookies and bubbles and sunlight streaming through the image in your head, and instead it's emergency-room visits, and sleepless nights, and whining that endures until your patience is gone.

Life Is What You Make It

Honestly, though, life is what you make it, and when you can let go of fear and accept the fact that life consists of a decent amount of hardship, you can enjoy the moments that are easy, and you can recognize the ways the hardship is building you. You can begin to savor your life and this short journey of motherhood, even with all the mess and mayhem that are just part of the package. Jesus warned us that life would be hard, but he asks us to be cheerful about it, knowing that he has overcome. "I have said these things to you, that in me you may have peace. In the world you will have tribulation. But take heart; I have overcome the world" (John 16:33).

But, we think, *what is the harm of a little complaining?* Why would God command us not to complain? It's easy to see when we look at our experiences with our own children. I've had children who struggle with this. We can be on an amazing family vacation, looking at buffalo in Yellowstone, enjoying picnics by the river, and they will complain about not stopping for ice cream. They are unaware of how hard my husband and I worked to make a magical day, and they only see what is missing. They can't see how much love we are trying to pour out on them, and our heart is grieved that they are missing the evidence of our great love for them.

I think God must feel the same way. He gives us beautiful sunsets, and hummingbirds that fly right in our faces, and children who are healthy, and then we complain about having to wash the laundry. He is daily pouring out love on us, saving us from untold disasters and providing our daily bread, and then we complain, and our complaints are so often about our actual blessings. I can remember the season of infants, the season many of you are in now, and the way that complaints about my own children could drip out of my mouth: "He won't take his nap," or "He whines constantly!" and "She pees the bed every night!"

Sometimes we need to share with our friends, and we need some empathy from ourselves and others, but when we make complaining a habit and fail to take our thoughts captive, refusing to find joy in our lives, we are shaping a worldview that can only lead to despair. In *Get Out of Your Head*, Jennie Allen writes (emphasis hers), **"What we think about, our brains become.** What we fixate on is neurologically who we will be." [4]

Complaining Changes Your Brain

When I was complaining about the hardship inherent in caring for a large family, or about our new life in Mexico, I was changing the structure of my brain and turning myself into an unhappy, fearful person. According to some research, complaining may shrink the hippocampus, an area of the brain critical to problem-solving, but it also releases the stress hormone cortisol, which lowers our immune response.

It's the same hormone released when we are afraid, having the same physical effect on our bodies.[5]

So not only does our complaining promote blindness to the blessings of God, but it is also killing us, releasing deadly stress hormones that open the door to other health ailments. When we give way to complaining, letting negative words spill out of our mouths like scentless vomit, we are creating scary, stress-filled environments for ourselves and those around us.

But how do we stop? Thankfulness, which we will discover more about in the following chapter, is one tool, but we start overcoming complaining and the fear that it breeds by taking our thoughts captive. Allen writes, "You and I have been equipped with power from God to tear down the strongholds in our minds, to destroy the lies that dominate our thought patterns. We have the power and authority to do this!"[6]

God has given us that authority, that ability to examine our thoughts and decide which ones are worth meditating on and agreeing with. "We destroy arguments and every lofty opinion raised against the knowledge of God, and take every thought captive to obey Christ" (2 Corinthians 10:5).

I didn't realize that I had this power while we were living in Mexico, and I was like the devil's rag doll, being dragged around by my emotions as I let them rule my life. Even though I read my Bible every day, I didn't realize that envisioning worst-case scenarios was acting contrary to God, and that by giving way to fear and complaining I was opposing the Word of God. I didn't know that I could take the thoughts in my head, and instead of agreeing with them, speaking them, and living by them, I could examine them and decide if they were true or not, and then act accordingly. In the Love After Marriage course, licensed marriage and family therapist Barry Byrne asks us to look at our emotions as temptations coming from outside of us instead of as feelings coming from the inside. He recalls a time when he began to grow angry with his wife after she had thrown his unread paper in the trash: "Suddenly the Holy Spirit spoke to me and said, 'This is a spirit of anger speaking to you, and the anger is trying to interpret your wife for you.' . . . As I prayed and put my thoughts in agreement with God's thoughts, my spirit changed. Nothing had changed in my circumstances, but my heart and my spirit had completely changed. I walked back in the house at peace."[7]

If I had been able to do this work of taking my thoughts captive during our time as missionaries in Mexico, it would have completely changed our trajectory. I could have examined the feelings and emotions as they came, and instead of letting them lead, I could have accepted some of them as valid, while others would have been kicked to the curb. If this perspective of examining my emotions and labeling them as truth or lie had been in my toolkit at the time, our home would have been happier, and our time as missionaries more life-giving.

Take Your Thoughts Captive

It's never too late to take your thoughts captive. It's never too late to put a stop to being the devil's plaything and to start letting God be the king of our mind, will, and emotions. I've lived through plenty of hard seasons since Mexico. I've moved to new communities, fixed up houses, been on my knees for struggling children; I've been the sole parent at home while my husband worked out of town, and I recently lived through a pandemic and subsequent lockdowns in California. I won't say that I never complain, but I now have "taking thoughts captive" skills that help me evaluate my thoughts and listen to the truth. Now when I'm feeling sad, mad, frustrated, discouraged, or scared, I take those thoughts to Jesus. I confess my struggles, I ask Jesus to cover me through his finished work on the cross and send any lies far from me, and I finish the prayer by asking him to tell me what is true. I might be reminded of a verse, or I might hear him whisper what is true, but the act of being quiet with God and acknowledging my struggle has transformed my life.

Beforehand, I would just give way to whatever I was feeling, but now I get to choose. I don't have to agree with fear. I don't have to make verbal agreements with believing the worst about God by complaining. I'm an adult, a child of God. I'm the beloved. That means I get to be the boss of my thoughts and words. I get to tell lies to go away, to tell fear, "Stop talking to me; I'm not listening anymore." I have the power to listen to the truth from God, instead of being moved by lies.

And overcoming complaining doesn't mean that we aren't allowed to feel. In *Try Softer*, counselor Aundi Kolber writes, "A significant part of learning to try softer comes from recognizing that old wounds may be causing us to live in fight/flight/fawn or freeze even once we're safe. . . . When I understand why my brain is reacting the way it is, I become empowered to validate the underlying need and then work on changing the situation."[8]

Kolber's book is full of insight into how our childhood wounds have impacted our ability to be whole adults. My own experience of being molested as a child caused me to believe that I wasn't loved, and that core lie opened the way for fear to speak to me. I used complaining as a way to be seen and noticed. I wanted sympathy and love. Because I was afraid that I wouldn't be cared for, I constantly let my husband know all that was wrong so he would give me the attention I craved.

It didn't work. My complaining led to a vicious cycle of fighting and stress in our marriage. It was a hard, hard season, but there was a silver lining. When my husband couldn't fix the core lie that nobody loved me, when my complaining failed to move him, I had no other option but to snuggle in close to God and let myself be loved by him. Once I took that lie captive and recognized how much God loved me, I was able to let go of my fears for the future and the complaining I was using to try to manipulate the present.

Maybe you've been relying on complaining to try to secure love for yourself. Maybe it's a habit you picked up as a child, or one that was born out of the intensity of parenting young children, but ask yourself, *Is complaining serving me? Is complaining securing the love I need?* Recognize that while it might serve as a relief valve, it's also raising your cortisol levels and making you blind to God's blessings.

So let's take complaining captive. In fact, let's take all these fears that are causing unrest and stealing joy from our homes, and together let's destroy them. If Ma could live through plagues of grasshoppers, fever and ague, near starvation, the loss of her home, living in a hole like a rabbit, and having her husband lost in a snowbank for days, then we can push through our own lives without giving way to

Let's take complaining captive. In fact, let's take all these fears that are causing unrest and stealing joy from our homes, and together let's destroy them.

complaining. As we do this, we aren't just making our own life happier and helping ourselves feel safer; we are giving our children a happier life and better chances for success. We are giving them grit, which is "firmness of mind or spirit: unyielding courage in the face of hardship or danger,"[9] the quality that helped people like Ma Ingalls survive her own life, and that can help your children thrive in the ever-changing world we live in.

According to studies by *Grit* author Angela Duckworth, this quality is a predictor of future success. "Across numerous contexts, one characteristic emerged as a significant predictor of success: grit."[10] When we cultivate grittiness in ourselves and our children, when we face each day with fortitude, we are giving our children the best possible chance at future happiness.

Our Children Are Watching

Ma might have been traversing her life without complaint because that's how she'd been taught, or she might have just been a really tough woman, but her fortitude was observed by her children and gave them the power to overcome hardship with grace. In *The Long Winter*, when Pa shares the news that the trains would not come through and the family would have to make do with the meager provisions at hand, Laura responds to his underlying message. "Laura knew what he meant. She was old enough now to stand by him and Ma in hard times. She must not worry; she must be cheerful and help to keep up all their spirits. So when Ma began to sing softly to Grace while she undressed her for bed, Laura joined in the song."[11]

Laura had been watching her parents, learning from the way they had navigated hardship, and now she was taking their cue. She was going to step up with them and push through the looming threat of starvation and stay cheerful for the sake of the younger children. Together, Ma and Pa and Laura and Mary were going to turn away from complaining and let a song of hope proceed from their mouths.

We can take this same path. We can overcome our fears and stay cheerful in the face of hardship. We can take our fearful, complaining thoughts captive and let a song of hope proceed from our own mouths. Our children are watching, and when they see us loving our lives, they experience that as love. When we are happy, they feel loved, but when we spend our days complaining, they will often feel responsible, feel that they are the cause of our unhappiness. They don't care all that much about their circumstances. They just want happy parents who will set the tone and help them feel secure—parents who live as those who are loved.

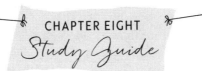

CHAPTER EIGHT
Study Guide

What are some of the thoughts, fears, and complaints you have been agreeing with?

Is complaining when you feel afraid helping you feel loved?

As you become aware of the thoughts, fears, and complaints that have been stealing your joy, pray this "1-2-3 Skidoo" prayer from Nothing Hidden Ministries:

1. *In Jesus' name, I nail to the cross_____ (fear, complaining, lies, etc.).*
2. *I break all agreements that I've made with this lie and I repent of joining with _____.*
3. *I ask you, Father, to send _____ (fear, complaining, lies, etc.) far away from me. And, Father, what do you want to give me in place of_____?*

Be quiet for a minute and listen. God may bring to mind a verse or whisper words of hope. This is what you can hold on to and turn to when fear tries to speak to you again.[12]

A VERSE TO MEMORIZE

These things I have spoken unto you, that in me ye might have peace. In the world ye shall have tribulation: but be of good cheer; I have overcome the world.

JOHN 16:33 KJV

MORE BOOKS ABOUT
Combating Complaining

To Read Aloud
LITTLE HOUSE ON THE PRAIRIE series by
Laura Ingalls Wilder
Mama's Bank Account by Kathryn Forbes
Pollyanna by Eleanor H. Porter

For Mom
Get Out of Your Head by Jennie Allen
Love After Marriage by Barry and Lori Byrne

9

Overcome the Fear of Not Having Enough through Thankfulness

The hand of God has led us here; we have set our shoulders to
the wheel, and we will not turn back.

Ralph Moody, *Little Britches*

In my earliest years as a new homeschool mom, I worked
to create a well-ordered life, beginning a fresh and exciting
adventure with each new school year. I set up the chalk-
board and the maps and gathered my children at our table
for lessons. Our schoolroom featured a big window so we
could watch the birds in the trees, and we warmed our space
with the heat from a wood stove. We picked up a few bookshelves from a big box store, thrifted some literature, and

kept learning together. Together we memorized Bible verses, read stories, and worked through spelling lists.

It was a simple, happy season. I was content with my home and my life and was doing my best to manage my growing family. My husband worked long hours at his job, so there wasn't much mental space for home improvement or fashion, but I didn't know how unfashionable I was or how unfancy my house was because my social circle was so small. Most of my friends were in similar situations, trying to care for young children, keep hardworking husbands fed, and if we were lucky, take a shower by ourselves. Life was simple and busy and good.

Fast-forward a few years, and my mental state was much different. I was now the mother of six children, living off-grid on a dirt road in Mexico, and making multiple emergency-room visits from this remote place. During this season, depression threatened to sink me. I started to question whether God loved me at all and started to wonder whether I could keep going. I was constantly looking back at the life I had lived before and feeling sorry for myself. I missed the tall trees and the clear lakes. I missed quiet walks down our lane through the many-colored leaves, and the peace and comfort we felt in that country home.

I was convinced that all my friends had easy lives, while I was the only one suffering. I felt it was unfair that I had to live in Tijuana, Mexico, where there wasn't even a Target, while friends from my old life lived near Anthropologie and Whole Foods. I was unhappy that we had only used furniture, while they had beautiful new dining tables and couches. I was depressed about my meager, used homeschool supplies, while they had closets full of amazing games and toys for their children. I was constantly comparing myself to others and feeling deprived. The sad thing is, I wasn't comparing myself to the many, many people who had it so much harder. I wasn't comparing myself to the migrant mama we met who was cooking lunch for her children over an open fire before putting them to bed in a broken-down van. I wasn't comparing myself to the homeschool mama I met in Mexico whose husband had been deported from the US for being there illegally and was now living an impoverished life in what to her was a foreign country.

My eyes were only on what I didn't have and what others did have. I was full of self-pity, feeling keenly the inconvenience of our off-grid life. We used a generator and wind power for electricity, so every usage had to be monitored. Every ordinary household chore was made harder by the lack of water and power. Laundry was never-ending with six children, and getting it done was a complicated multistep process:

Step 1: Check to see if we had enough water in the tank.
Step 2: Start the generator (if we had enough gas to run it).
Step 3: Start the washer.
Step 4: Hang the laundry on the foggy coastal hillside and hope it would dry before we ran out of clothes.

Nothing was easy, and I missed my comfortable American existence. When we moved into the off-grid house, my sixth baby was just eight weeks old, and the home lacked a few basics. My husband had built it with the help of local contractors and volunteers, but we were tired of paying for a rental on the United States side of the border and moved in before it was technically livable. We had a toilet in a shed, no running water, no heat, no refrigeration, and as mentioned, no electricity. We brushed everyone's teeth that first night with bottled water, used flashlights to find our way to bed, and cuddled under the covers to watch *The Andy Griffith Show* until the battery on our computer died.

I felt alone in my struggles. My friends from California were all living such normal lives, but I found a mama who could understand what I was going through and who could guide me. I found a mama who also had to move to a difficult situation but who could find the silver lining. When Mother from *Little Britches* first spotted the home they had moved to from the eastern United States, she must have felt dismay. It was an old cottage hauled from Denver out to the Colorado prairie, and the first sight of the shack they were to call home was devastating. The windows were smashed, the plaster had fallen off the walls and ceiling, and it was all Mother could do not to cry. Instead she said, "The Bible says, 'Trust in the Lord and do good; so shalt thou dwell in the land, and verily thou shalt be fed.' The hand of God has led us here, we have set our shoulders to the wheel, and we will not turn back."[1]

I wish my attitude had been similarly hopeful. How different that period in my life could have been! Throughout the LITTLE BRITCHES series, Mother had to face hardships that most of us cannot imagine: crawling across the prairie in the middle of storm winds while trying to keep her kids from blowing away, losing the ranch, losing her husband, nearly dying of blood poisoning, almost losing a child to measles. Her life was hard—much, much harder than mine—but her character was beautiful.

Throughout my life, I had lived in fear of not having enough, comparing myself with friends who had more. A friend once told me, "You have the worst case of FOMO I have ever seen." Fear of missing out, of being less than, had sabotaged my character and stolen joy. The battle with comparison and fear of lack had plagued me my whole life. During my teen years, I compared myself to friends I thought were prettier. During the early years of marriage, I compared myself with friends who had a better wardrobe, and during the early years of motherhood, I compared myself with friends whose children were better behaved. Then, during the missionary years, I was constantly looking over the border at friends whose lives were more leisurely, whose homes were prettier, and whose husbands were less adventurous.

Finally, this all came to a head after we moved to that house in Mexico. Books have been teachers for me, and the example of Mother from *Little Britches* was giving me perspective, while Ann Voskamp's *One Thousand Gifts* was giving me strategy.

In Everything Give Thanks

During that hard season, when so many normal routines were made extra difficult by our lack of electricity and our limited water supply, I read about the practice of giving thanks—even for small and seemingly insignificant things—and it became a lifeline for me. I started giving thanks for hot soapy water for washing dishes, and for the baby butterfly bush at the front step that benefited from the used dishwater. I gave thanks for the stunning ocean sunsets we viewed over the dusty Baja hills, and for clean laundry—even if it took days to get it done. This practice helped me appreciate the small blessings in my life. As I recognized these precious gifts, I began to shake off fear and come alive.

In her book *One Thousand Gifts*, Ann Voskamp writes, "This living a lifestyle of intentional gratitude became an unintentional test in the trustworthiness of God—and in counting blessings I stumbled upon the way out of fear."[2]

It was this acknowledgment of beauty and goodness in my life that brought freedom from fear. This active giving of thanks was key to unlocking joy. As I looked at the shining eyes of my own child or the vivid sunset out my front window instead of at the perfect lives I imagined my friends were living, strength came. I was able to shake off fear and live full of wonder at the miracle of life.

> It was this acknowledgment of beauty and goodness in my life that brought freedom from fear. This active giving of thanks was key to unlocking joy.

You might be fighting this same battle with the fear of not having enough. Comparison might be stealing your joy and making it impossible to enjoy the fleeting years with your children. For many of you, the battle is made worse by social media. When I was a younger mom dealing with this issue, I had only my real-life glimpses into the homes of a few friends to compare with, but now we can peek into the homes of millions of mothers, and they all seem to have more than we do: a more diligent workout routine, more beautiful eco linen clothing, a more stunning kitchen. It's even more intense when we are homeschooling. We are constantly exposed to moms who are better crafters, moms whose children do better notebook pages, moms using a new curriculum, moms who take nature walks every day. All of this exposure to the highlight reels of millions of moms can leave us feeling inadequate in a hundred different ways: *I'm not crafty enough,* or *I don't have money to make my kitchen as pretty as hers*, and *I can't buy the newest linen apron.*

It's like we've all bitten the apple from the Tree of the Knowledge of Good and Evil. Before social media, we didn't know what skincare product a given influencer was using, or what shoes they were buying, or that everyone else had a brand-name leather couch. We know too much now, and it can drive a sense of inferiority, leaving us feeling less than, lacking, and lost.

Keep Your Focus Small

But the LITTLE BRITCHES series offered me a different way of looking at life. All this mother wanted was her family, and despite the many hardships in her life, she was thankful. She spent her precious free time reading aloud to them, and she savored the time with her family. After the ranch they had worked so hard to build was lost, Mother was still found reading aloud to her children, creating happy holidays, and doing what was needed to keep the family together. She built bonds that would stand the test of time. Even when the main character of the books, her son Ralph, was far from home, he was thinking of her, sending her letters, and doing his best to support her. Her investment into loving her children and keeping her family together after the loss of her husband meant that her children wanted to be there for her as well. She kept her focus and her world small, and that created contentment.

I think that is one of the keys for us as well. When we can hyper-focus on all that we do have and make our world a little smaller, we will find more love for ourselves and our lives. Voskamp writes,

How my eyes see, perspective, is my key to enter His gates. I can only do so with thanksgiving. . . . And if I can give thanks for the good things, the hard things, the absolute everything, I can enter the gates to glory. Living in His presence is fullness of joy—and seeing shows the way in. The art of deep seeing makes gratitude possible. And it is the art of gratitude that makes joy possible.[3]

Isn't this what we are after? More joy? More freedom from fear and more enjoyment of our lives, our homes, our marriages, our children, ourselves? I believe that it is this shrunken perspective, this narrowed view of the world that makes this possible. When we stop looking all around us, at everything we don't have and everything others have, we can begin to love our own lives. When we, like Mother in *Little Britches*, keep our focus on the small daily blessings in our own small worlds, we will find new joy.

For some, this might require shutting down social media altogether, pulling the plug on the constant stream of advertising marketed as community. For others, it might mean deleting just a few accounts that are especially triggering. If an account instantly makes you feel that there is something you don't have or causes FOMO or a sense of inferiority, it might be worth unfollowing. After all, your joy, and your enjoyment of your life, aren't worth sacrificing for some virtual inspiration. Our "chief end is to glorify God, and to enjoy him forever,"[4] and if we aren't enjoying him, it might be that we are moving too fast to notice his goodness.

Maybe for you it's not social media that is driving the fear of lack, the comparison, and its related misery. Maybe all you need is a simple perspective shift. Voskamp suggests taking time each day to write down three things you are thankful for. In my work supplying homeschool resources at the Peaceful Press, I created a planner with space for recording thankfulness (available at thepeacefulpreschool.com/the -homeschool-planner), recognizing that when we see all the beauty in our lives, we can overcome fear and gain joy. As you begin to note all the blessings in your life, taking the time to see and memorialize them, your sense of richness will grow. Instead of feeling that you don't have enough, you will see all that you do have. Instead of thinking that God is not for you or good to you, you will be able to see all the kindness he has shown you.

Where It Begins—and Ends

For so much of my life, I didn't believe that God loved me, so it was easy to feel inferior, like an orphan child just hoping to be noticed. But when I internalized the truth that he has loved me "with an everlasting love" (Jeremiah 31:3), I began to love myself. In *Gentle and Lowly*, Dane Ortlund writes of God's love for us, "Even the most intense of human love is but the faintest echo of heaven's cascading abundance. His heartful thoughts for you outstrip what you can conceive. He intends to restore you into the radiant resplendence for which you were created."[5]

Before I understood this, I was trying to restore myself by adding things—brand-name clothes, mothering prowess, a nice car—all in an effort to make myself lovable. The core issue that was driving the fear of not having enough was the fear that I wasn't loved. When I began to see myself as the beloved of God, for whom he lives to intercede, I found that I no longer needed externals to make me something. I was loved just as I was: no makeup, slightly flabby, emotional, and lacking in self-control, logic, and wealth. I didn't need to add anything. I was loved, I was loved, I was loved.

And you are loved. Nothing you can buy or do can make you more lovable. God made you, and he loves you. You are precious to him right now, just as you are. You can let go of fear and comparison and just rest in that sufficiency. You can relax into contentment, knowing there is nothing missing, nothing broken. Knowing that you are loved can help you have eyes wide open to the many ways God is daily showing his love for you.

As the story of *Little Britches* comes to a close, the family has suffered many setbacks, but they are still trusting in the goodness and love of God. When Mother hears about how Father gets a needed promotion at work, the way they see the situation says much about where they put their hope:

> Father looked up and smiled. "Yes Mame, that means—" he said, "that he made me boss carpenter. I'm getting four dollars a day, and I know I can make a good job of it." He took a couple more mouthfuls and then he looked up again. "How does that line near the end of Hamlet go? The one about there being a divinity."
>
> Mother knew them all, I guess. She got tears in her eyes and in her voice, too. "There's a divinity that shapes our ends, rough-hew them how we will," she repeated.
>
> Father nodded, "That's the one. How do you remember them all, Mame?"[6]

It seems that knowing God is in control and is trustworthy, that there is a "divinity that shapes our ends," is what kept Mother and Father hopeful and content even in the worst of circumstances. And as I learned to be content in whatever situation I found myself, as I learned to count my blessings, my contentment grew. I learned to avert my eyes from those things that stole contentment and focus on the truth that God was for me. I began to live as the beloved.

But comparison is a sneaky little devil, and even when you think you've shut all the doors, it will still find an air vent or a window to creep in. As I was writing this chapter about how I had overcome the fear of not having enough, I stopped to check my email and saw a note from a fellow writer. She was describing the gala she put on for her children, and I instantly started thinking about how I probably wasn't as good a mother as she because I hadn't planned any parties this season for my children, and I wasn't making enough happy memories for them. Despite the fact that we take hikes by mountain creeks every week and stop for ice cream nearly as often, that we sit around the table for dinner nearly every night and make seasonal bucket lists we try to fulfill, I felt inadequate. Comparison was trying to push its way back in. Even when we've awakened to the beauty of our lives and have started listing all that we have to be thankful for, it can try to find another way to convince us that we are deficient.

> I learned to avert my eyes from those things that stole contentment and focus on the truth that God was for me. I began to live as the beloved.

I think we sometimes have the mistaken idea that growth is a one-time event. We think we can overcome an issue, and it will never bother us again, but growth is a process. I overcame my young adult fear of comparison centered around not having pretty clothes, or tan skin, or a fit body. Yet that same fear recreated itself in my early mothering years as comparison over who was a better mother, and then emerged in my middle mothering years as the fear of not giving my children a happy childhood.

In your own battle with comparison-related fears, endurance is needed. Even as you avert your eyes from all the beautiful products on social media, you may find yourself comparing other aspects of life: whose children read more books, whose children play instruments with more proficiency, which mother has read all six volumes of Charlotte Mason's HOME EDUCATION SERIES. If we don't get the core question *Am I lovable?* settled, comparison will reinvent itself and keep bobbing back up to the surface like a sturdy little cork. We settle this question as a daily practice when we cultivate thankfulness, because it is a way to come alive to the love of God. When we are thankful, we are observing and acknowledging the truth that God cares for us. God commands us to be "giving thanks always for all things unto God" (Ephesians 5:20 KJV), not because he needs to hear us say thank you all day long, but because our thankfulness is an acknowledgment of how loved we are. When I do something nice for my son, like take him to the creek to tube down the icy rapids, and then for ice cream after, I want to hear him say thank you—not because I'm hungry for praise but because his thanks reflect his awareness that he is loved. When we as God's children cultivate thankfulness, even for small daily blessings like running water, we are cultivating awareness that we are loved, and we are conquering fear.

In his brief poem "Evening," G. K. Chesterton appreciates and ponders God's gift to him of another day during which he has "eyes, ears, hands"[7] and as he contemplates the offering of the same tomorrow, he wonders at the great blessing of being allowed another such day.

This poem reminds me to take stock of my blessings, to have eyes wide open to even the littlest hints of God's love and care for me. It can be a reminder to you also. All of us have something to be thankful for. As many things as might be going wrong in your life, there are always gifts as well. We just have to be looking for and counting our blessings.

At the very end of *Little Britches*, after Father has died, after Mother has survived blood poisoning, and the remaining members of the family are finally safe at home together, Ralph Moody describes their supper:

> That first supper was the most memorable meal of my life. The big yellow mixing bowl sat in the middle of the table, filled to the brim with well-browned pieces of chicken, stewed until it was almost ready to fall off the bones, whole potatoes, and carrots—with big puffy dumplings, mixed at the bedside, floating on top.
>
> Father had always said grace before meals; always the same twenty-five words, and the ritual was always the same. Mother would look around the table to see that everything was in readiness; then she would nod to Father. That night she nodded to me, and I became a man.[8]

Mother had learned the words of Job, "The LORD gave, and the LORD hath taken away; blessed be the name of the LORD" (Job 1:21 KJV). When, by all accounts, her life was a ruin, Mother blessed the Lord, and she gifted her children with grace. Her thankfulness was the sword she wielded to push away fear, and we can wield this powerful sword too. When we keep a daily account of all we have to be thankful for, and take it a step further to let our children know that we are grateful for them, we create a culture of contentment. We are helping them see the world as a place of abundance, a home with a very good Daddy who provides for all our needs. When we reject comparison and the fear that we are not enough and instead model thankfulness, despite the difficulty of our circumstances, we remind them that there is a God who loves us. We demonstrate to our children and to the world that there is a God who is with us, and in whose presence is fullness of joy.

CHAPTER NINE
Study Guide

How have you compared yourself with others?

How has God helped you overcome?

List three blessings in your life. Make this thankfulness list a daily practice.

A VERSE TO MEMORIZE

Write down this verse and work on memorizing it.

Giving thanks always for all things unto God and the Father in the name of our Lord Jesus Christ.

EPHESIANS 5:20 KJV

MORE BOOKS ABOUT
Thankfulness

To Read Aloud

The Family Under the Bridge by
Natalie Savage Carlson
Little Britches by Ralph Moody
Man of the Family by Ralph Moody
A Single Shard by Linda Sue Park
Amos Fortune, Free Man by Elizabeth Yates

For Mom

One Thousand Gifts by Ann Voskamp
Ruthless Trust by Brennan Manning

Overcome the Fear of Not Being Able to Manage by Building Good Habits

Now, suddenly, she wasn't afraid anymore, because there was nothing to be afraid of.

Frank B. Gilbreth and Ernestine Gilbreth Carey,
Cheaper by the Dozen

I had my seven children over a span of fifteen years, and the parenting pendulum swung wildly as the years passed. When my first few children were born, I thought I knew everything, and I cobbled together my own parenting method that was an uneasy mix of Tedd Tripp's *Shepherding a Child's Heart* and the Waldorf method.[1] I wanted the structure and obedience of the first parenting style while still nurturing a love for nature, creativity, and individuality in my children. To satisfy the structure side, I created a color-coded schedule for myself and my children in thirty-minute increments. Each color block represented a new activity that I would manage. Everything was on that schedule: chores, reading time, and school subjects. To fulfill my longing for creativity and nature, we took long walks in our quiet Northern California forest, cared for beloved family pets, and sat by our bubbling creek reading aloud while the sun danced on our faces, and I provided free access to craft supplies so creativity could be expressed. While I fought through fears as I added new babies and navigated caring for multiple children, I started to find my groove and dedicated myself to the sacred journey of motherhood.

Change Contributes to Chaos

My confidence was shaken by our experience as missionaries in Mexico, and by the time we moved back to the United States to have our seventh child, I felt like I was on an eternal obstacle course. I'd get one area of my life in order, and then someone else would have a crisis; the obstacles just kept coming, with no breaks to take a breath. And there were a lot of troubles. My sixth child was born via emergency C-section, which required months of recovery. When she was six weeks old, we moved to the aforementioned house in Mexico—our sixth move in two years. Added to that were the other medical crises we had gone through: my oldest child bleeding from the throat after a routine tonsillectomy, my second child experiencing a week of seizures, and my sixth child having a fifteen-minute febrile seizure.

We had a slew of terrifying and disorienting experiences in the years preceding this seventh child, and they created an ideal environment for fear to flourish. As we endured each new move, medical crisis, and meltdown, I felt like a small boat in a vast sea, clinging to the rope for safety until things calmed down.

It's no wonder that I no longer felt confident in managing my family by the time I had this last baby. It's not astonishing that fear had started to creep in and tell me that I was failing as a mother, that I couldn't really create the home atmosphere I longed for. We had endured so much hardship in our missionary adventure, and rapid change can leave anyone gasping for breath as they try to find equilibrium again.

But my habit of reading aloud was still a constant, even in all the turmoil. We read every morning and nearly every night, and as we settled back into life in the United States, I—having left as the mother of five and returned as the mother of seven—read the book *Cheaper by the Dozen* aloud to my children. And inspiration came.

Cheaper by the Dozen is the true story of the Gilbreth family; the parents, Frank and Lillian Gilbreth, were motion study experts during the age of factories in the 1920s. Their occupation was observing mechanized industrial workplaces to discover wasted time and movement, with the goal of creating efficient factory environments. Their job might seem dry, but the telling of their family story by two of the children is heartwarming and hilarious. It also gave me fresh inspiration for overcoming the fear that I couldn't manage.

As I read *Cheaper by the Dozen* and saw how this family kept learning new things and holding on to healthy routines and rhythms, I realized that habits can be an antidote to fear.

When we start to feel that we can't manage and begin enter-taining fearful thoughts of the impact of our inadequacy, we create a self-perpetuating cycle: The fear causes us to freeze, and the more we do nothing, the more chaotic our life becomes. The Gilbreths certainly had their share of chaos. The whole family came down with the measles, they moved several times, and they added a new baby nearly every year for many years, but they kept up their daily habits, adding more as time passed, and gained new skills in the process. The writers described their family routines:

> Dad installed process and work charts in the bathrooms. Every child old enough to write . . . was required to ini-tial the charts in the morning after he had brushed his teeth, taken a bath, combed his hair, and made his bed. At night, each child had to weigh himself, plot the figure on a graph, and initial the process charts again after he had done his homework, washed his hands and face, and brushed his teeth.[2]

We laughed our way through it, but as I read, hope that I could overcome fear and nurture my own large family flooded my heart. If they could manage twelve children, surely I could manage seven! I returned to the good habits I had developed when we were a smaller family, and life was more predictable. We started with simple things like making our beds every day and keeping our rooms tidy. We added cleaning the kitchen before going to bed at night, and daily walks in nature. Morning time, when we read aloud from the Bible and literature, was a constant through the years, but we needed to add habits that made our world feel more manageable and reduced squabbling. When simple tasks such as picking up bedrooms at the end of a day or taking out the trash are daily habits, we don't have to scramble or fight to get our kids to do them. And with each new habit we worked on, my world became more peacefully productive, and my confidence grew. Charlotte Mason wrote of habits, "Every day, every hour, the parents are either passively or actively forming those habits in their children upon which, more than upon anything else, future character and conduct depend."[3]

This concept that I'm either developing bad or good habits in myself and my children was a loud wake-up call. It's reasonable to give ourselves some grace when we are in a season of deep anxiety, but we cultivate fear in our homes when we descend into chaos. Children feel safer and more comfortable when the world is predictable. When I made simple daily habits a priority (getting dressed, brushing my teeth, making my bed, morning time with my kids), I was creating a happy atmosphere for my children where they could confidently try new things. The more we pushed back on the chaos trying to conquer us, the more time we had for crafts, or baking, or hikes in the woods.

Habits Can Help

Maybe you've gone through a season of change when life feels out of control. Whether it's a move, or a job change, or a new baby, small and large changes can throw us off and make us feel disoriented, opening the door for fear as we scramble to find our footing. Maybe you have felt like me, at one time confident and capable but rendered faltering and feeble after a slew of unfortunate events. Hard times may have left you upside-down in your ability to create a peaceful home. Now you are seeing the effects of the chaotic environment on your children.

That was the worst part of my battle with the fear that I couldn't manage—seeing the insecurity it caused my children. It wasn't a huge fear that I was dealing with, but as I left my post as leader and let my household try to run itself, it caused stress and confusion for my children. When I began to create some healthy structure, it helped my children relax and learn. Their joy increased as my fear decreased. If we, at the very least, can haul ourselves out of the fetal position to make our beds, brush our teeth, and change into comfy clothes for the day, and ask our children to do the same, we are creating a safe and secure environment for our families. And as we push through our fear and lethargy to help them develop good habits, we are carving out a peaceable kingdom in a very crazy world.

While sometimes we are managing a little fear and it's just a simple matter of getting back to our daily habits, there are times when the weight of fear feels extraordinarily heavy. I've felt that way during most significant changes, like our move to Mexico, with each new baby, and then the pandemic that sparked an entirely new struggle with fear. In our most difficult times, those seasons when fear threatens to strangle us and leave us incapacitated and impotent, habits can be the hedge that keeps us going. George MacDonald put it this way: "Fold the arms of thy faith, and wait in the quietness until light goes up in thy darkness. Fold the arms of thy Faith I say, but not of thy Action: bethink thee of something that thou oughtest to do, and go to do it, if it be but the sweeping of a room, or the preparing of a meal, or a visit to a friend."[4]

When we were living in Mexico, and I realized that I was courting depression, I read a little book by John Piper called *When the Darkness Will Not Lift*. In the book, he quotes this sermon excerpt by MacDonald and encourages us to simply do the next thing—to get in motion.

This advice empowered me to go for a walk through the sagebrush with my children when all I felt like doing was sitting on the couch feeling sorry for myself. It empowered me to read a book aloud when it would have been easier to hide in my room. It empowered me to help my children develop their own daily habits instead of just staying in bed. When fear was trying to keep me helpless, habits were the key to walking in authority over my own life, and they can be a guardrail for you as well. When you have a habit of reading one picture book aloud to your children every morning or taking a walk every afternoon, those habits can be part of a system that keeps you moving forward in your life, capturing joy, and running after purpose, despite how you feel.

James Clear, the author of a favorite book on habits called *Atomic Habits*, writes,

> Habits are like the atoms of our lives. Each one is a fundamental unit that contributes to your overall improvement. At first, these tiny routines seem insignificant, but they build on each other and fuel bigger wins that multiply to a degree that far outweighs the cost of their initial investment. They are both small and mighty. This is the meaning of the phrase *atomic habits*—a regular practice or routine that is not only small and easy to do, but also the source of incredible power; a component of the system of compound growth.[5]

So when you start and maintain habits, you are being incredibly powerful in your own life. You are telling fear, "You don't rule me." When you get up every day and drink your coffee, make your bed, and put on clothes again (even the same clothes your baby spit up on yesterday), you are a queen. You are a woman who is ruling her castle and ruling over fear. And your children can feel the security and safety of the castle you are building one good habit at a time.

With daily habits of self-care, morning time, and loving our homes, we disempower the devil and continue our work of bringing order and beauty into the world, despite our emotions. James Clear articulates this well: "Habits form based on frequency."[6] Even difficult habits can become easy when we are consistent, when we continue doing them day after day. As we stay consistent in doing the next right thing, we change our mood and the world one small step at a time.

Habits as a Hedge

For the Gilbreth family in *Cheaper by the Dozen*, habits weren't just their everyday systems. Habits were the hedge that kept them going after a tragic loss. When the circumstances of life became so intense that separation (placing the younger children with relatives) threatened the family, the systems and habits that were in place kept them functional even when their parents couldn't be present. Habits kept them together. These systems and rhythms helped keep children fed, laundry clean, meals on the table, and homework done, even when both mother and father were out of the picture through illness or work. In a season when the children might have been afraid and disoriented, the habits their parents modeled were a safety net, preserving their joy even in the worst of circumstances. Habits saved their family from fragmentation.

Practical Steps for Habit Building

But how do we start cultivating good habits when we have no experience? Some of us were raised by working mothers in a sort of free-for-all where structure was never modeled. My mother worked full-time during most of my adolescent years, and my daily after-school habit was to turn on the television and get a snack until about five minutes before she was due home, at which time I would frantically start doing the dishes. I had very few self-management skills, my upbringing and personality converging in a self-centered and moody package that took no thought of making the world a better place. My routine was to get up, go to school, come home, watch TV, do the dishes, go to bed. I didn't have good habits that helped me to work toward a goal or to create a better life for myself. I just lived in the moment.

When I became a stay-at-home mother, I had to learn to choose how I would spend my days. Would I lie on the couch and watch shows all day, or would I get up and vacuum the floors? Would I have playdates every day, leaving my home in chaos until tomorrow, or would I make the beds and do the dishes before we left for the day? I had to "boss myself" because there was nobody to tell me what to do. The only way to overcome the fear that I couldn't manage was to start managing. I had to face the fear and do it anyway.

Doing what needs to be done despite our emotions, and in the process building good habits, is one of the greatest predictors of success and happiness for our children. James Clear writes further about the connection between delayed gratification and success in life, explaining, "This is precisely what the research has shown. People who are better at delaying gratification have higher SAT scores, lower levels of substance abuse, lower likelihood of obesity, better responses to stress, and superior social skills."[7]

We know that we need good habits to help us overcome fear, especially the fear of not being able to manage, but how do we start? And how do we keep going? For me, there were three steps to creating good habits.

Make a Plan

Amid the chaos and intensity of raising small children, we often don't even have mental space to think about good habits. We are just trying to survive, to get enough sleep, to keep these small humans alive. The problem is that if nothing is written down and we keep spending our days on crisis management, the crisis will follow us even when life circumstances get calmer. So start with a simple plan. Maybe just write down one, two, or three things you will do each day. For example: (1) Make my bed. (2) Brush my teeth. (3) Start one load of laundry.

If you can start with a simple task list and tackle that in small increments, you will soon find mental space to tackle more. When you get that space, make a master list. Make a list of all the things you need to do and want to do. Your list could look something like this:

Exercise
Take a nature walk
Read aloud
Organize a closet

Read the Bible
Try a new recipe
Mop the floor
Take a nap
Laundry
Dishes
Plant a garden
Look at Instagram
Potty train the toddler
Learn to knit
Teach a math lesson
Have lunch with a friend
Organize bookshelves
Read a book
Teach a child to read
Organize toys
Shop

When you have a complete list of all the things you need to do each day and even some things you want to do, you can start to automate your good habits and even reward yourself for accomplishments. Instead of just doing what you feel like every day, check a couple of things off your list and then reward yourself by doing one of the fun things. Make your habit-building a delight.

Track Your Habits

Over the past year, I've joined several challenges with a few other moms. We even hosted one in the Peaceful Press group that helped us track homeschool habits such as morning time and nature walks and paying attention to mama self-care. When we are busy loving our children, we can forget to love ourselves, and so reminders to drink water, take our vitamins, and get enough sleep are essential also. *Atomic Habits* author Clear reminds us of this, "Habit tracking provides visual proof of your hard work—a subtle reminder of how far you've come."[8]

I've created charts for myself and my children, hung our Peaceful Press Chore Cards (picture-based prompts for preschool habit building available at thepeacefulpress.shop/products/the-peaceful-press-chore-and-routine-pack) in prominent places, and joined challenges in an effort to track my habits, knowing that when I have visual cues I am more likely to accomplish what I have set out to do.

Find Your People

As I was writing this book, I started a text group with a friend who was also working on a writing project. I also joined a writing group on Facebook that offered accountability through daily check-ins. In my early days of motherhood, we belonged to a church that was full of supportive parents, and my friend circle was full of homeschoolers. Having these social groups with shared values helped support my desire to nurture my family. Joining a group that affirms your personal goals is a powerful way to combat fear and live into your purpose. When I was afraid that I couldn't homeschool, I had friends to reassure me that it would be fine. When I was scared of having a large family, I had friends from large families who encouraged me in that journey. I overcame many of my parenting fears through the help of my friends.

When fear threatens to paralyze us, the power of community can keep us moving forward and creating the life we dream of. You probably have friends who offer moral support and accountability as well, but if you haven't found them yet, start searching. Find a Peaceful Press family through our Facebook group or a Wild + Free group at www.bewild andfree.org; look for a church where your values are supported or join an online community for accountability. The dreams you have for your family, even the ones that scare you, aren't out of reach, but you do need a friend to run with.

Maybe you've been so incapacitated by fear that you aren't even sure what habits to start. Life with children is busy, and we slip into survival mode so quickly, just existing instead of growing. I hosted a habit-themed giveaway on my Instagram, where followers shared a habit they are working on in the comments as part of their entry. Some of the comments inspired me; maybe they can offer you a spark also.

> When fear threatens to paralyze us, the power of community can keep us moving forward and creating the life we dream of.

Meg: "I just had our third child—my other two are almost 5 and almost 2—and the habit I've been working on is setting out their breakfast and clothes for the day the night before. They're then able to get up, get dressed, and eat breakfast, even if I'm still in bed nursing the baby. Sanity saving!"

Rachelle: "Working on a consistent morning routine with my two oldest. Breakfast then chores then school—we have a new baby in the house and our routine kind of went out the window the first few weeks but we're getting back into the swing of things."

Michaela: "I'm working on saying 'yes' more, to the little things that may not be the most convenient but that help me build relationships with my little ones."

Kayla: "Trying to get into the habit of having my kids help with chores rather than just doing it all myself."

Brittany: "Pausing quietly prior to immediately reacting to frustrating happenings. A 'cool down' moment."

Katie: "Chores! We have a system, but it went out the window when I had a baby seven months ago. Starting to get back into being consistent again."

You can see that you aren't alone in feeling overwhelmed and anxious about managing your family. Mothering is tough at any stage, but when you prioritize establishing good habits and work at it little by little, you will be able to craft a life of joy and beauty for you and your children.

At the end of *Cheaper by the Dozen*, the family faces the untimely death of their beloved father, but he had lived to prepare them for this day.

The bad heart was one of the principal reasons for Dad's home instruction programs. It was also why he had organized the house on an efficiency basis, so that it would operate smoothly without supervision; so that the older children would be responsible for the younger ones. He knew a load was going to be thrown on Mother, and he wanted to lessen it as much as he could.[9]

Although he knew that his heart was bad, this father didn't let fear of the future paralyze him and keep him from loving his family. He gave it his all, preparing them for life and helping them know they were loved. We hope to never have to face the loss of a loved one, but the truth is that life is a fragile gift; we can't predict the future, and neither should we live in fear of it. Instead let's build little habits that push back on paralyzing fears. Let's give it our all, pouring out love on our children and preparing them for life.

While the father didn't seem to be afraid of anything, the mother had dealt constantly with fear, according to the children.

> While Dad lived, Mother was afraid of fast driving, of airplanes, of walking alone at night. When there was lightning, she went in a dark closet and held her ears. When things went wrong at dinner, she sometimes burst into tears and had to leave the table. She made public speeches, but she dreaded them. Now, suddenly, she wasn't afraid any more, because there was nothing to be afraid of. Now nothing could upset her because the thing that mattered most had been upset.[10]

It took the loss of her husband for Mama Gilbreth to overcome her fear, but we can do better. Let's not wait for a tragedy to become brave. Let's put on courage now, build some good habits, and create safe harbors for our children in a world full of turmoil. As we build good habits into our daily routine, we create time to enjoy our life. By pushing back on debilitating fear and creating the tracks for home management to run on, we make time to craft with our kids, or spend the day in nature, or sit by the fire reading aloud, or even just read to ourselves. Habits help us push back the fear and fall in love with our life, one baby step at a time.

CHAPTER TEN

Study Guide

When you feel afraid, what is your normal reaction?

What are three habits you want to start building to push back fear?

Who are three friends you can ask to hold you accountable?

What is one thing you will reward yourself with when you have kept a habit going for three weeks?

A VERSE TO MEMORIZE

Fear not, for I am with you;
  be not dismayed, for I am your God;
I will strengthen you, I will help you,
  I will uphold you with my righteous right hand.

ISAIAH 41:10

MORE BOOKS ABOUT
Managing with Good Habits

To Read Aloud
Mama's Bank Account by Kathryn Forbes
Mary Emma and Company by Ralph Moody
The Boxcar Children by Gertrude Chandler Warner

For Mom
Atomic Habits by James Clear
A Mother's Rule of Life by Holly Pierlot
Little Men by Louisa May Alcott

Overcome Fear by Running after Purpose

LITERATURE COMPANION: *Freedom Train*

She was not afraid. She would return to the land of bondage and set her people free.

Dorothy Sterling, *Freedom Train*

We moved a lot. My husband carried me over the threshold of our first home right after we said our "I do's." This apartment was where I first burned spaghetti for my parents, where we first decided television was not for us, and where we began to dream of our own family. We only stayed a year, moving to another apartment, then to the duplex where we planted our first garden and brought home our first child. There were several subsequent homes, but when the drama of Y2K was building, we decided it was the right time to find the country home of our dreams. After many weekends spent driving dusty country roads in an old green van that my husband thought we could live in (an idea that was quickly tabled), we finally found what we could afford. The house wasn't much to speak of, but it was where some of the happiest memories of our lives were made. We stayed there for several years before moving to Mexico, and in just four years as missionaries, we moved six times.

A Move to Regret

I regret several of those moves; uprooting your family always has a cost, but the one that preceded the darkest time our family had ever experienced was the move to the rodent house. After our missionary adventure in Mexico, we had settled into our life back in the little house with the creek and the happy memories of simpler times, but when my husband's company started sending him out of town for work, he began a job search, wanting to be home at night with his family. One of the places he had done contract work for was a power line in the mountains a few hours south of our home, and it was a place that captured his imagination. He had worked in Yosemite as a young man, and this historic powerhouse on the road to Yosemite became the focus of his job aspirations. He applied, completed the required tests, and then waited and prayed. Meanwhile at home, I was doing my best to be cheerful while parenting solo much of the time, as my husband worked out of town.

One incident that summer seemed minor, but the effect on our lives was traumatic. My oldest daughter was hiking and rappelling in a mountain canyon with friends, and as she braced herself against the face of a cliff, a boulder the size of a bowling ball came hurtling down, crashing into her thigh and ripping the skin deeply. She had to hike two miles out of the canyon to get back to the cars, and I panicked when I got the call that she had been injured. When I got to the hospital, she was calmly powering through the pain as the doctors cleaned her up and sutured the wound. Unfortunately, the injury led to an infection that required strong antibiotics, and when she recovered from that, she was suffering from something much worse.

In the meantime, we were still praying hard for this new job for my husband; on the morning of his birthday, we asked God to answer our prayer for the job offer. Later that day as I was browsing the Target aisles with four of my children, my husband called me, the emotion evident in his voice. He had gotten a call from human resources and was to start his dream job the next month.

While we were rejoicing about the new job, we were beginning to fear for our daughter. Her injury and subsequent weight loss led to a few quiet discussions between us, during which she complained about being fat. I tried to reassure her that there was no shred of truth in that statement. Inwardly I was growing afraid, but I was also very preoccupied with the move we were about to undertake. Just two short years after we had trucked our belongings from Mexico to the Northern California foothills where we still had a home, we would have to move again.

With my husband starting work in a new town, we needed to find a house, and I was fearful about the impact on my oldest daughter. She had gone through so much loss in the last several years, giving up a horse to move to Mexico, giving up an identity as a missionary kid to move home, losing a beloved dog to a tragic accident. She'd been given a new horse when we moved back, and I was determined to find a house that would allow her to keep it. I didn't want to perpetuate more loss in her life. I couldn't avoid the move, but I was willing to do anything in my power to halt the slide into disordered eating and depression I was witnessing in my beloved daughter.

Fixer-Uppers and Fear

We finally found a place we could call home. It needed work, but it provided the most room for our large family (and the horse) that we could find in our price range, so we put in an offer and prepared to move. The house had a convoluted floor plan with hallways through bathrooms and an awkward little shower in the master and a cavernous shower in the hall bath, but there were several mature fruit trees, a lilac bush, and a family room that would provide space for a schoolroom. Many times during the process of buying that house, we second-guessed ourselves; the house had been abandoned for a year, and there was ample evidence of a rodent infestation. However, our family had suffered enough separation because of my husband's job, and we were desperate to be together again. We pushed through our fear and misgivings to purchase the house.

The younger children were excited about the move. The house seemed novel with its odd hallways, enormous shower, and interesting cupboards. The property was overgrown and derelict, starving horses had chewed through the barn wood, and the pond was full of cattails, providing a fake bottom that nearly drowned our own well-fed horse in our first few months there. Despite its derelict condition, the new home felt like a big adventure to the younger children as they explored its mysteries.

As I worked with my tireless older daughter to settle into this new home, I tried to encourage her, but I could see a deep weariness beginning to strangle her. We continued cleaning and deodorizing and painting, trying to rid the house of the fetid smell of mouse urine as we simultaneously tried to pull our beloved daughter from the grips of anorexia. I started quietly reading books on the subject and looking for counseling, but there was no clear path to take. This was to become a desperate time, much more frightening than anything we had experienced in Mexico.

My hardworking and stable oldest daughter, who just months before was helping me run the house while my husband was working out of town, had disappeared, and in her place was an underweight and depressed child who would cook elaborate meals and then refuse to eat them.

Christmas was especially frightening. When we woke in the morning, we realized that we didn't have enough powdered sugar for our cinnamon roll frosting and asked her to drive to the store to purchase some. She was gone a long time, and the thought started to run through my mind that perhaps she had run away—or worse. We drove to the store to check on her, discovering that the opening time was later than we had expected, and she was safe. Her behavior had gotten so erratic, and I felt utterly at a loss regarding how to help her. Terror was a constant companion as we searched for answers.

Finding Hope When All Seems Hopeless

I didn't even know where to start with finding support. The homeschool community we had been a part of in Northern California was sweet, but they all seemed so perfect that I feared they would judge and reject me if they knew what was really going on. I tried finding counseling for my daughter, read every book I could get my hands on, prayed for answers, and begged for a breakthrough. I just wanted my daughter back.

That was a long, weary season. As winter faded into spring, we were still struggling to find answers and professional help. During this devastating season, I read *Eating with Your Anorexic* by Laura Collins, and it was a lifeline for me. I felt like I had found a friend, a counselor, and answers all at once. Sadly, finding answers didn't make the depression my daughter was dealing with go away; as she headed off to work at a summer camp, the situation got even more intense. She was working with people she loved, but early in the summer, while she was still clawing her way out of depression, the daughter of the camp leaders disappeared. She also had been dealing with depression, and after an outpatient therapy appointment, she simply walked off and wasn't heard from again. The whole camp turned out to look for her, my daughter included, while I was back at home consumed with worry and trying to be present with my six younger children. My beloved daughter was already fighting for hope, and now the camp that had seemed like a safe place where she could be nurtured by mature Christians was in the middle of a desperate search for a suicidal teen.

It was the teen's mother who finally discovered her. Hanging from a tree, her body already in the early stages of decay, she was gone. I was devastated for the mother, knowing how easily it could have been my daughter, and terror continued to grip me as I prayed for healing. The book of Lamentations was my meditation at that time. "Through the LORD's mercies we are not consumed, because His compassions fail not. They are new every morning" (Lamentations 3:22–23 NKJV). I staggered through that summer, praying my heart out and living in fear, my heart in my throat much of the time as I pleaded for my daughter's life, health, and well-being.

Harriet Shows Me the Way through Hardship

I hope none of you will be in the situation of having a depressed or suicidal child, but we will all have seasons that threaten to do us in. Whether because of marriage problems, sick children, financial setbacks, or our own mental health issues, there will be times when we just have to keep plodding forward, putting one foot in front of the other as we wait for the light to break through. We all will have periods in our life that we don't think we can survive, when grit and endurance will be our lifeline. Seasons of hardship are just a part of life, but our books can show us the way.

Harriet Tubman was a slave in the American Antebellum South who knew the pain and the power of endurance. As I read *Freedom Train* by Dorothy Sterling aloud to my children, I was given a picture of what sacrificial perseverance looks like, of what pushing through fear for the sake of others means. Harriet wasn't content just to gain her own freedom; she risked her life countless times to secure the freedom of her people. She waded through icy cold rivers, navigated swamps, and hid in cemeteries to save her people from a life of slavery.

Harriet must have grown weary at times, desperate to see the chains break and her people go free, and desperate for release from the difficult life she was leading. Still, her love for them overwhelmed her weariness, compelling her to keep running toward freedom. When one of the Underground

Railroad organizers tried to warn her of the dangers of helping her people, she responded, "I been doing men's work all my life. I'm not afraid."[1] He believed her. "She was not afraid. She would return to the land of bondage and set her people free. In his journal . . . he wrote, 'She seems wholly devoid of personal fear. The idea of being captured by slave hunters or slaveholders seems to never enter her mind.'"[2]

Her love for her people proved greater than her fear, and love empowered her to return again and again to secure their freedom.

Love Is the Answer

I believe love is the key to how we must navigate terrifying times as well. We won't have the endurance to keep trusting that light will break through unless we are truly compelled by love. In John 15:13, Jesus says, "Greater love has no one than this, that someone lay down his life for his friends." Love compelled Harriet to action. She didn't wait around for someone to come and help her, and she didn't look to other people to take care of her and her people. She pushed through fear and did what was in front of her to do, and in the process led three hundred people to freedom. But she didn't stop there. When the Civil War began, Harriet then offered her services to the Union army, ultimately becoming a liaison to the newly freed slaves. "'Most of the people are

> As I read **Freedom Train** aloud to my children, I was given a picture of what sacrificial perseverance looks like, of what pushing through fear for the sake of others means.

very destitute, almost naked,' Harriet dictated in her first letter to Boston friends. 'I am trying to find places for those able to work and provide for them as best I can, while at the same time they learn to respect themselves by earning their own living.'"[3]

Harriet loved her people, and love is action. She traversed the Southern states to organize classes in washing, cooking, and sewing. She taught women who had worked in the fields their entire lives how to take care of a home and to create marketable goods. With her own paltry earnings, she set up a community washhouse where the women could earn money washing uniforms. In an effort to avert jealousy because of her special treatment, she gave up her meals in the army mess hall—meals she earned by working tirelessly for the Union army. At the end of each day, she went back to her cabin to bake pies and brew casks of root beer that newly freed slaves could sell to the soldiers to provide for their needs.

Love Is Action

Harriet put her love in action, and as I read about her life, I was inspired to action in my own home. Instead of continuing to wander around in fear as I waited for a breakthrough for my daughter, I started taking action to bring joy to my family. We had picnics in the fields of our new house, replicating those at our beloved former home. We hosted spring parties with chocolate eggs hidden in the grass (also modeled on previous happy times), with tables set up for children to color hard-boiled eggs while we mothers chatted together about the joy and pain of parenting. I taught a preschool class, playing with letters and numbers with a few adorable little children, and hosted a homeschool co-op where my science-loving boys dissected a frog, thanks to a loving friend with a stronger stomach than mine.

Despite the difficulties we were going through, love was an action we did, not just an emotion we felt, and it made all the difference in our home. In her book *Awaking Wonder*, Sally Clarkson emphasized this. "Love exercised, words of encouragement and affirmation, respect given, appreciation verbalized are fuel to human hearts and minds. Love is the air that we breathe in to support the rest of life's demands. Love provides an invisible support system that gives mysterious strength and health to live well in the day-to-day demands."[4]

Love was mine to give, namely because I was a grateful recipient of it. I wasn't trying to love from an empty, grasping place, but from an overflow. Because of my experience in Mexico and the fight I'd gone through to know the love of God, I was able to keep loving my family even when I was afraid. I wasn't waiting around for someone to love me, to show me I was loved. I already knew that I was loved. My beautiful Jesus had revealed his love to me, which gave me the power to pour out to my family as I navigated long and scary days of parenting teens in crisis, while cuddling my toddler, and playing with glitter glue with my preschooler, and gathering around great books for morning time, and canning peaches from the tree on my patio. The well of love was full and was renewed daily, which empowered me to do the work of loving without complaint.

First John 4:16 illustrates this: "So we have come to know and to believe the love that God has for us. God is love, and whoever abides in love abides in God, and God abides in him."

I had come to know and believe the love God had for me. It was no longer a far-off concept, and I was no longer tempted to believe that God hated me or that he couldn't be trusted. The work I had done thus far to overcome fear—the grieving, the forgiveness, and the "taking thoughts captive"— had burned up that lie. I was able to trust in God's love for me, which empowered me to love my family even when they weren't very lovable.

This truth that at the very core of fear is the lie that we aren't loved is worth repeating because it's easy for us to slip back into it. When we feel unloved, when we believe this lie, we are driven to self-protection and to grasping to meet our own needs. I think Harriet, as a child in her parents' home, must have been made aware of the reality of God's love, and that this translated into faith that God would come through for her. Her daddy, Ben, would take her for a walk every Sunday, showing her the natural wonders where they lived, teaching her to navigate by the moss on the trees and the stars in the skies—unwittingly preparing her for her destiny. The songs they sang in the camps told of their trust in God, "Didn't my Lord deliver Daniel? And why not every man?" Harriet didn't let the horrors of slavery embitter her toward God, but instead kept trusting in his power to deliver. As she lay dying, she sang, "Swing low, sweet chariot, coming for to carry me home,"[5] knowing that her Deliverer was indeed coming to take her to glory.

But how can we shake off the fear and the lie that we aren't loved? How do we get out of our head and quit imagining the worst? How can we keep living in love? Our children need us. They need our presence. They need to see us smiling and laughing so they can believe all will be well in the world. It's essential that we shake off the fear, but it's easier said than done, and often we need to repeat the same steps and continue running the race, even when we are still dogged by fear.

It's not a single-step process, but one that requires grit to keep taking our thoughts captive and forgiving those who trespass against us. It's a practice of daily reminding ourselves of the truth from the Word of God that we are loved. It's not a race we run once and win, but a purpose we go after. It wasn't enough for Harriet to make one trip to free her people. She kept going, until the war was won and her Father called her home. She was running after purpose, compelled by love, and she didn't quit until she took her last breath.

We need this kind of endurance. We need to keep repeating the process. Just as we pray the Lord's Prayer daily, we repeat the steps for overcoming fear as needed, keeping our weapons at hand so we can win the battle and prepare our children to win as well.

So much is at stake. My fears for my children caused me to lose time with them, instead of being present and modeling the way through fear. My own mother's fears for her children had the same impact on my siblings and me. Our desperation to keep our families safe and to help them grow up and do well actually had the opposite effect, as it created a fearful atmosphere that squashed creativity, bravery, and love. It's like fear could smell itself and moved in close to taunt us with our own thoughts, ultimately stealing away precious time with our children.

We Overcome through Love

But I am overcoming, and you've got what it takes to overcome as well. The same Spirit that raised Christ from the dead lives inside of you and me (Romans 8:11), and we've got access to all the power we need to rise above fear and live with all the passion and purpose we were made for. We can be part of that great cloud of witnesses, overcoming the fears and self-doubt that come against us and loving our children. We can teach them to laugh in the face of fear, to find joy even when the days are dark, and to live for a purpose that is higher than themselves. Instead of sheltering our children from the storms of life, we can outfit them with these same tools so they can live a life of purpose and joy, even in hard circumstances.

> We can teach our children to laugh in the face of fear, to find joy even when the days are dark, and to live for a purpose that is higher than themselves.

Just as God's glory was displayed to the Israelites as he opened up a path through the sea and destroyed their enemies, just as his glory was displayed through Harriet, who was empowered to lead her people to freedom despite a traumatic brain injury, his glory will be displayed in us as we run the race with endurance.

> Therefore, since we are surrounded by so great a cloud of witnesses, let us also lay aside every weight, and sin which clings so closely, and let us run with endurance the race that is set before us, looking to Jesus, the founder and perfecter of our faith, who for the joy that was set before him endured the cross, despising the shame, and is seated at the right hand of the throne of God.
>
> Hebrews 12:1–2

Let us run the race with joy, and for the joy that is before us and all around us. Let us fill our children's lives with joy and love; let's conquer fear and live free.

CHAPTER ELEVEN
Study Guide

What compels you to keep caring for your family even when you are afraid?

What steps in the fight to overcome fear have you taken? Circle all that apply to you:

Forgiving
Grieving
Taking your thoughts captive
Meditating on Scripture
Developing good habits
Developing a family culture
Writing down your essentials
Singing

Which steps in the fight to overcome fear do you still need to take?

A VERSE TO MEMORIZE

Herein is love, not that we loved God, but that he loved us, and sent his Son to be the propitiation for our sins. Beloved, if God so loved us, we ought also to love one another.

1 JOHN 4:10–11 KJV

MORE BOOKS ABOUT
Fighting Fear with Love

To Read Aloud
Amos Fortune, Free Man by Elizabeth Yates
Up from Slavery by Booker T. Washington

For Mom
How to Stop the Pain by James B. Richards
Lies Women Believe by Nancy DeMoss Wolgemuth

Overcome the Fear of Leading through Forgiveness

LITERATURE COMPANION: *Endurance*

Shackleton was concerned. Of all their enemies—the cold, the ice, the sea—he feared none more than demoralization.

Alfred Lansing, *Endurance: Shackleton's Incredible Voyage*

Motherhood wasn't something I spent a lot of time thinking about as a young woman. I wanted a boyfriend and I wanted to make money, but I can't remember daydreaming about babies or thinking much about what would become such a defining part of my life.

When I had been married a few years, my sister had her first child, and suddenly my maternal desires kicked in. I had my first child when I was just twenty years old, and we added another one nearly every two years for the next fifteen years. Someone asked me once if I'd planned to have seven children, and in truth I had to tell them no. Initially, I leaned toward a smaller family. I didn't want to have more kids than I could love well, but as each new child came, my love grew. Delighted with my role as a mother, I passionately threw myself into caring for my children. I was confident I could do better than my own parents and protect my children from the misery I had experienced as a rebellious teenager. I thought that if I could just order their world perfectly and train them well, they would grow up without the pain and entanglement of shame and regret. They could be unencumbered by memories of failed relationships, their brain space wouldn't be taken up with demeaning song lyrics, and their consciences would be undefiled by lies.

I thought that it was in my power to prevent the world from entering my home. I wanted to create a safe space where sin would not tempt them and where they could stay clear of the mistakes their father and I experienced as children of the eighties, whose parents looked away far too often. I thought that if I was caring enough and watchful enough, diligent and consistent enough, then my children could rise above the world and be perfect, even as our Father in heaven is perfect. And many of the parenting books I read nurtured this false hope. Books like *Growing Kids God's Way*, *Shepherding a Child's Heart*, and *To Train Up a Child* seemed to convey the idea that if we parents would be diligent enough in raising our children, then they would be arrows, shooting straight at their heavenly mark, with no human error to deter them from their course—never mind that most of the authors still had young children when they wrote these books, and with the waters of choice as yet untested, free will hadn't yet marred their doors. Don't get me wrong; these books had some worthwhile ideas. It's great to teach children to listen to their parents, to be respectful of adults, to be mindful of consequences, but the message I took from these books was that if I simply followed the rules, then my children would be happy, healthy, and godly; in short, they would be perfect. But pride goes before a fall, and my confidence in my ability to raise perfect children, as well as my lack of understanding of humanity, was to be the rock I stumbled on.

In spite of this, those early years with my children were happy and holy. We were active in our church, and we were diligent parents. We took family mission trips to Mexico and camping trips to the mountains, building happy memories as we played and served together. We sang, and read aloud, and planted gardens together, and created a life-giving home. But simmering under the surface was the poison of pride and misguided faith in my power to produce perfection. I was confident in my ability to lead my little flock, and I felt sure that I knew what I was doing—until I didn't.

After sixteen years of being a "perfect family," enduring the stress of missionary life and leaning too heavily on my oldest daughter to carry me through that stressful season, it all fell apart. As we struggled to help my daughter overcome disordered eating and depression, my grand illusions of control were shattered. This sparked a massive identity crisis for me. I thought that I could be a perfect mother and produce perfect children who would not be the victims of lies. I thought that if I just protected them with enough tenacity, they would reach adulthood unstained by the world.

The perfection bubble burst, though, and left me feeling naked and afraid, like a shipwrecked captain in a boat that was far too small. My faith in myself as a leader was destroyed, and I found myself paralyzed as a parent, terrified that I would make more mistakes with my younger children. Fear led me to abdicate my role as a parent, to reject the authority of the Bible as a guide, and to begin a haphazard search for answers. I couldn't pinpoint what mistakes had led to my daughter's disordered eating, but fear of making the wrong move and bitterness toward bad leaders debilitated me as a mom.

Maybe you are feeling the same confusion and paralysis as a mom. You might have set out with a clear idea of how to parent and then discovered your child was on the autism spectrum, presenting a whole new set of circumstances. Maybe you observed your parents and, fearful of imitating their mistakes, tried an opposite approach as a parent.

For me, trying to move forward was a monumental struggle. I had six younger children; in the mix were toddlers, elementary-aged children, and a daughter with special needs, and here I was with my oldest child, my "test subject," falling apart. I had poured so much effort into parenting well and being a good mama, and the struggle that she was having shattered me. I became convinced that her struggle resulted from my perfectionist parenting. Because of this, I sat back for a season—too long—and let my younger children find their own way. In my lack of confidence, I let the two-year-old take over and try his hand at bossing the rest of us around.

As any of you know who have a two-year-old, they are very good at telling people what to do, but not so good at thinking about others, and the longer I let him be a tiny tyrant, the less my other children enjoyed him—and the less they respected me. I'm not saying that I let him take over on purpose, but I did start experimenting with an opposite parenting style. Instead of going back to the Bible and examining my mothering in light of the Word, in my despair I threw the baby out with the muddy bathwater. I decided that my emphasis on character training had contributed to the eating disorder, so instead I made everything about love, choices, and acceptance. Those things have their place, but there is a reason God gave the Israelites the commandments before he gave them Jesus. If there weren't any rules to break, and no opportunity to feel remorse, there wouldn't be a need for grace. When we offer acceptance without accountability and full autonomy for children whose brains aren't developed enough to understand the consequences of their actions, we stunt their growth and ultimately create an even more scary atmosphere for us and our children.

But I'm a slow learner, and I let this experiment of giving my younger children choices about everything have free rein for a time. I gave them the option to argue, persuade, and overrule me as I waded through these feelings of failure. My fear of making a mistake as a parent and the despair I felt at seeing my child struggle caused me to change tack and cause even greater harm. Disrespect grew in my older children as they saw me manipulated by the younger ones, and fear rose in the youngest as he felt the insecurity of being a small person with too much power. I kept up our homeschool routines, but I lacked the moral authority to say no and stick to it, or to give directions and make sure they were followed. The older children already had good habits of speaking respectfully and being courteous, but I was failing to instill basic civility in the youngest while I was stuck in regret. I kept reading parenting books to try to understand what was going wrong, but as you probably already know, it was literature that threw a light on the situation. And this time I wasn't learning from a sweet mother, but instead, a gruff adventurer.

Ernest Shackleton was a British explorer who dreamed of traversing the final frontier, Antarctica. He had been an officer on Robert Falcon Scott's race to the South Pole, but when Roald Amundsen became the first man to reach that icy destination, he set his sights on a bigger project. He decided that instead of merely reaching the South Pole, he would take a crew of men and sled dogs and cross that frozen uncharted wasteland, meeting up with another ship of men who were waiting on the other side.

I learned from him as I read *Endurance: Shackleton's Incredible Voyage* aloud to my children while living through family chaos. I read it while I felt incapacitated as a mother, full of self-loathing over my perceived mistakes. I read it during a season when I had abdicated my role as captain of my home. Books are always informing our lives, even when we are unaware. I wasn't reading the book as a character lesson; at the time it just seemed like a fascinating story to share with my adventurous children. But reading this book reformed my thinking in a way that a parenting book never could. Instead of someone telling me what to do or providing a list of tips, I observed leadership in action and contrasted it with the lack of leadership in my own home. Understanding the impact good leadership makes on a crew, whether it's a crew of sailors or a crew of children, helped me snap out of my mama malaise and take back the helm of my home. It was the wake-up call I needed to start leading my little flock again.

But what was so instructive about this story? The fact that it's one of the greatest survival stories of all time is surely part of the intrigue, and reading about how Shackleton and his first mate, Frank Wild, led their crew out of disaster transformed my mindset, giving me hope that I too could overcome fear and learn to lead again.

Shackleton sailed to Antarctica with a plan to leave the ship with a few sailors on board and set out across the frozen continent with dog sleds. Instead, the ship froze right into the Weddell Sea, far from their desired drop-off point, which forced them to abandon their ambitious plan. They spent a whole winter locked into the ice like a rock in a frozen pond. That in itself would have driven most of us mad. We think "stay at home" orders during the COVID-19 crisis were bad, when we still had Instacart and Amazon at our beck and call, not to mention about a million shows to distract us from the situation. These guys had nothing but their ship's rations and each other. It was Antarctica, so most of the winter was spent in darkness. When they finally decided to abandon the sinking ship and make their way back to civilization with two small boats, they were well aware of how impossible their situation was. They had to camp out on ice floes at night, and during the day push the two heavy boats across the ice until they could find open water. The discomforts they suffered were many, and I'm sure there was a temptation on every man's part to just give up and die—and if Shackleton led like I had been doing, that is precisely what would have happened.

> Understanding the impact good leadership makes on a crew, whether it's a crew of sailors or a crew of children, helped me snap out of my mama malaise and take back the helm of my home.

I had been letting my shame about the mistakes I had made and the fear of making new mistakes keep me from moving forward as a mother. But inspired by Shackleton, I observed how he got his men through their horrible situation and started imagining how he would lead. Instead of just throwing up my hands and giving up, I pushed through the fear and despair and started mothering again.

So what was this magic formula that saved these men from an icy death?

Shackleton Kept Going

Whether he had made a miscalculation as a leader or it was just a fluke of bad weather, twenty-seven men were in a desperate situation. When Shackleton finally gave the order, "She's going, boys, I think it's time to get off,"[1] as the ship sank slowly into the frozen waters, he must have felt hopeless. However, we never really know what he was feeling because he didn't let feelings guide him. He held himself together to lead his men, despite his mistakes. He kept moving forward. In fact, some of the time he might have been giving orders just for movement to keep up morale.

As mothers, there is so much we can learn from this strategy. When we are in a hard season, when our fears and emotions threaten to sink us, and we cannot provide leadership, we need to simply give our kids something to do. Perhaps it's a season when you make a different choice for their schooling, or maybe you tag team with a sister who takes the helm for the day. Perhaps you set out craft supplies and let them entertain themselves while you figure yourself out. Or you organize a cleaning party and follow up to make sure tasks are completed. Perhaps you take a picnic lunch to a favorite nature spot and let them run wild. Fear and despair will try to sink us, but finding ways to keep your crew moving while you figure out what to do next can mean all the difference for little people who aren't ready to be in charge.

Shackleton Made Time for Fun

As we explored in an earlier chapter, sometimes fear can make us dull and dry, keeping us constantly in our heads, worrying instead of remaining present with our kids. I'm sure Shackleton was worried, trying to work out a way to get home, despite the impossible situation. "In all the world there is no desolation more complete than the polar night. It is a return to the Ice Age—no warmth, no life, no movement."[2]

They had just survived a polar winter, which was enough to drive anyone mad, and now they had to make their way across the ice and seas to get home. The crew of another ship that was beset in the Weddell Sea ice several years before the Shackleton expedition is described: "With the coming of the night, the *Belgica's* crew became infected with a strange melancholy. As the weeks went by this slowly deepened into depression and then despair. . . . In order to offset the terrifying symptoms of insanity they saw in themselves, they took to walking in a circle around the ship."[3]

In my favorite account of the expedition, author Alfred Lansing contrasts the experience of the *Belgica* crew with the *Endurance* crew: "But there was very little depression on board the *Endurance*. The coming of the polar night somehow drew the men closer together."[4]

One of the reasons the *Endurance* crew was able to fight off depression is because their captain made sure there was the *element of surprise*, a phrase I learned from Julie

Bogart's book *The Brave Learner*. Even though the four walls, or two in the case of a ship, never changed, they had creative diversions that kept their minds intact. They held recitation nights, when every crew member could recite poetry and verse, and had their Saturday evening grog to look forward to; they also enjoyed Sunday evening music concerts when one crew member would crank away at the phonograph while the others listened or wrote in their diaries. They played pranks on each other and put on plays and in so doing, diverted themselves from the horrors of their situation.

I'm not advocating for escapism here—I think modern Americans are already too adept at that—but I am calling on us as mothers to create joy even when we are afraid. I'm calling on us to throw a party, or put out some play dough, or make root beer floats, or just do something to distract ourselves and our children from our fear. Sometimes we can't change a situation, but if Shackleton could inject fun into a polar shipwreck, we can certainly inject a little fun into our own situation.

Routines and Rhythms and Action

We talked a lot about the importance of routine and rhythm in a previous chapter, but it's worth mentioning again. In *Cheaper by the Dozen*, the family made it through the devastating loss of their father through their attention to good habits, and the disciplined life that the seamen of the *Endurance* lived helped carry them through their own terrifying circumstances. In fact, inaction was perceived as their enemy. Shackleton grew concerned when they had been stranded on the ice for a few months after abandoning ship. He had kept his men busy with regular mealtimes, exercise, hunting, and repairing clothing. These rhythms had kept them going, had created a flow to their days that protected their mental health and outlook even amid such perilous circumstances. But they couldn't just sit there on the ice floes forever, and inaction was leading to discouragement. "Shackleton was concerned. Of all their enemies—the cold, the ice, the sea—he feared none more than demoralization. On December 19, he wrote in his diary: 'Am thinking of starting off for the west.'"[5]

When we are afraid, our routines and rhythms can be the wheels that ease our way forward, especially when we have something to look forward to. Settling into apathy and inaction can be the easy path, but it's certainly not the path through fear. As the popular slogan and book title says, "Feel the fear and do it anyway." We have to keep going. Maybe for you that means starting a new exercise regimen or taking a daily walk with your kids. For some moms, the way forward is to join a Bible study or book club, overcoming fear through community. Even in the scariest of situations, forward movement and working toward goals through daily disciplines can be a hedge that provides a feeling of safety and of hope.

Forgiveness Is the Key

One thing I discovered as I studied the life of Shackleton and worked through my own fears was that unforgiveness was a link keeping me and fear chained tightly together. Holding on to grudges toward my parents for their mistakes caused me to fear repeating those mistakes with my children. Holding on to grudges toward people whose advice didn't work for us caused me to swing too wide in the opposite direction.

Finally, holding on to grudges toward myself for my mistakes as a mom was debilitating. I've seen this same scenario play out in some of my friends. They think their parents are too strict, so they throw all rules to the wind with their own children. They are angry with the leaders who gave their parents bad advice, so they swing to the opposite side of the spectrum. As these moms grow older, and their own children start to struggle, they feel the weight of guilt as witnesses to these struggles and give up. They just stop trying.

Have you hit that wall as well? Have you exhausted your reserves of wonder and made the decision to throw in the towel? Are you feeling the heaviness of disappointment in your children and yourself, and are you afraid of making a wrong move—or simply frozen with fear? I've been in that place. When I began my mothering journey, I thought I knew everything, and fear was not a looming presence in my life. But as my children grew, I began to understand how impossible it is to guarantee outcomes and to ensure their safety. Fear of making a mistake, of having failed them, even fear of the future began to boom loudly in my ear. It was a paralyzing voice, keeping me stuck and immovable, afraid to step out and lead.

But then there was Shackleton. His men followed him, even initially to their detriment, because he was going somewhere. It was said of him, "This indomitable self-confidence of Shackleton's took the form of optimism. . . . It set men's souls on fire; as Macklin said, just to be in his presence was an experience. It was what made Shackleton so great a leader."[6]

But how could I get myself going again? How could I break through this sludge of mistakes that was keeping me locked down and scared? How could I get a fresh start?

It was forgiveness that set me free. It's a simple Bible principle and one I thought I was walking in, but I found a new way to look at it when attending a Nothing Hidden Ministries marriage workshop. Praying the Lord's Prayer was a regular occurrence for us, including, "Forgive us our trespasses as we forgive those who trespass against us," so I knew forgiveness was something God wants us to make a daily practice. Even so, I didn't realize how powerful active forgiveness could be. In the workshop we attended, they didn't just ask us to say "I forgive you" to people who had hurt us. It went much deeper than that.

To start with, we were to forgive people even if they weren't coming to us and asking for forgiveness. In Katherine Schwarzenegger Pratt's *The Gift of Forgiveness*, she shares how people who have experienced unimaginable abuse and pain are able to heal through forgiveness. DeVon Franklin is one of these people. His dad was an alcoholic who died when DeVon was just nine years old, and DeVon carried the wounds of anger and self-pity with him, which was sabotaging his adult relationships. "'The challenge about not offering forgiveness,' DeVon says, 'is that many times the person who has offended has moved on with their life, for better or worse. But the one who is offended holds on to the pain in ways that can be severely detrimental to the entire course of their life.'"[7]

DeVon's dad was never going to come to him and ask for forgiveness, but when DeVon offered it to him anyway, he was able to move past the pain and build a life for himself.

It's important to God that we forgive. There is a saying that "bitterness is like drinking poison and waiting for your enemy to die." But I think Jesus expresses it more clearly, "For if you forgive others their trespasses [their reckless and willful sins], your heavenly Father will also forgive you. But if you do not forgive others [nurturing your hurt and anger with the result that it interferes with your relationship with God], then your Father will not forgive your trespasses" (Matthew 6:14–15 AMP).

When we hold on to grudges, thinking that people deserve our anger, we aren't hurting the object of our anger. We are only hurting ourselves. In *The Gift of Forgiveness*, contributor Cora Jakes Coleman expresses it this way: "Forgiveness isn't about the person who's betraying you or lying to you or denying you; forgiveness, for me, is about me taking my power back and not allowing them to affect me emotionally."[8]

Active forgiveness is a gift to ourselves. It helps us to move forward in freedom, instead of being held back by the pain of the past. But active forgiveness isn't just saying "I forgive you" to the air. The practice that I learned went much deeper than that, and it has become a regular part of my life. As things come up for me, or when I notice that I'm getting offended, I take some alone time to process what happened. I might even take time to grieve it, a practice we talked about in chapter 2. When I'm ready, I'll take time to pray a forgiveness prayer, thanking God for his mercy toward me as a way of opening the conversation with him, then forgiving the offender in return.

But I don't stop there. I go on to list out the ways they hurt me and the emotions I felt. As I give myself permission to acknowledge the pain of that incident, it cuts me free from the chains that would keep me stuck in that broken moment. Thoroughly forgiving my own parents has set me free to be a better parent. Thoroughly forgiving the man who molested me as a child set me free to be a victor and not a victim. And when I thoroughly forgave myself for the mistakes I had made as a parent, I was set free to begin again. I was free to restart my journey with all the hope and optimism of my early days of motherhood, and with the belief that "as far as the east is from the west, God had removed my mistakes from me" (Psalm 103:12 paraphrased).

Freedom is a wonderful feeling. It's what gives us the ability to paint with our children instead of judging ourselves for not being good enough. It gives us the power to run playfully through the woods with them instead of feeling embarrassed of what people might think. Freedom from fear opens new doors to creativity and joy as we unfurl our tattered wings and begin to fly. It's what gave me the confidence to sit beside a gifted artist and let her teach me how to hold a brush. It's what gave me the confidence to fashion a flower crown and put it on my head, even if there were ten other flower crowns more lovely than mine. Forgiveness opens the door to freedom and gives us the power to get back behind the helm of our own little ship and follow through with our crew on even the simple tasks, like bed-making and baking and music practice and memory making. Forgiveness frees us to recapture our own childhood, to become the carefree and creative girls we once were, even as we delight in the season with our children. Forgiveness disempowers the fear of making mistakes and frees us to love our children and our lives with ferocity and joy.

> Forgiveness disempowers the fear of making mistakes and frees us to love our children and our lives with ferocity and joy.

I think this childlike optimism and freedom from self-reproach empowered Shackleton to lead so well. When his expedition had essentially failed, and his ship had sunk, he kept going. He kept leading his men, sacrificing his personal comfort to ensure theirs and making decisions that kept them busy and hopeful. It's one of the greatest survival stories ever. Against all odds, not one man died during that desperate dash from the ice floes of Antarctica to South Georgia Island, amid the most treacherous waters on the planet.

We aren't all called to lead through these kinds of treacherous experiences, but as mothers we are all called to lead. Children need captains, not shipmates, and as we make forgiveness a daily practice, as we make accepting and extending the grace of God a regular part of our life, we can keep ourselves free and fast and full of life for ourselves and our children.

CHAPTER TWELVE
Study Guide

In what ways has a fear of making mistakes robbed you of leadership abilities?

How have you overcompensated to make up for the mistakes of your parents?

Make a list of people who have hurt you and then work through the following tool:

1. First, say a prayer thanking God for his forgiveness and asserting that because you have been forgiven you choose to forgive (insert person's name here).

2. Now list the ways you've been hurt by this person (for example, the abandonment or loneliness you felt, being uncared for or misunderstood). Include the ways this affected your life—the way the actions of this person impacted your relationships and opened a door for further pain. Take time to really acknowledge all that was lost because of their actions so you can leave it in the past.

3. Next, say a prayer of blessing over them, asking God to help them live in a way that doesn't harm others.

4. Finally, take time to forgive yourself for the mistakes you have made and the pain those mistakes have caused you and your family. Be thorough so you can be free.

A VERSE TO MEMORIZE

If you, O Lord, should mark iniquities,
O Lord, who could stand?
But with you there is forgiveness,
that you may be feared.

PSALM 130:3-4

MORE BOOKS TO INSPIRE
Overcoming, Leadership, and Forgiveness

To Read Aloud
A Single Shard by Linda Sue Park
The Secret Garden by Frances Hodgson Burnett
Shackleton's Journey by William Grill

For Mom
The Gift of Forgiveness by
Katherine Schwarzenegger Pratt
Evidence Not Seen by Darlene Deibler Rose
Unbroken by Laura Hillenbrand
Love After Marriage by Barry and Lori Byrne

Overcome Fear by Knowing Scripture

LITERATURE COMPANION: *The Hiding Place*

> The blacker the night around us grew, the brighter and truer and more beautiful burned the word of God.
>
> Corrie ten Boom, *The Hiding Place*

They say March comes in like a lamb and goes out like a lion, but in 2020, "lion" felt a little too mild to describe what we experienced. The month started so sweet with a trip to San Diego to learn something new while my husband and children explored Disneyland. But the world shifted gears very quickly. As we drove the eight hours home, news of a pandemic started pouring in. Countries shut their borders to protect people from a deadly virus, and the world went into panic mode.

The border closing felt especially dramatic in my home. My seventy-year-old dad was in a village in Romania recuperating from a budget-friendly hernia surgery, and my daughter was a law student in Northern Ireland. They were far away across the Atlantic, and we wanted them home with us. Finally, after many frantic phone calls with airlines, they found flights and made their way across the ocean until everyone was safely ensconced at home. I had all seven of my children, along with my parents, quarantined together in our small home when our state governor announced the stay-at-home orders, closing all nonessential businesses until further notice.

I was thankful. There was a lot of cooking and cleaning, and with extra guests, personal space was a luxury not easily found. But as I thought about the difficulties of the past winter when our septic system failed and we were forced to carry our dishwater out in buckets for a month as we worked on repairs, I was acutely aware of how much worse it could be.

And then it did get worse. The rain began to stream down from the heavens, and the pressure valve on the septic opened up in my yard like a vulgar little party popper. Used toilet paper erupted, spilling onto the purple asters that grew near the ground. A day later, my youngest son sprained his ankle at a time when nobody wanted to be in the emergency room. We simply iced it and dodged a figurative bullet (a trip to the emergency room in the midst of COVID felt very scary), until the next morning when I awoke to my stoic husband moaning and writhing on the floor. We took him to the emergency room, where after four hours and several thousand dollars, we found that he had kidney stones. So there we were, repairing our septic system and bucketing our water, my husband in agony, my youngest child limping around, and a houseful of people to feed and care for. I wearily pushed through, even as fear found new ways to speak to me.

I had overcome so much fear in my life—the fear of what people thought of me, the fear of managing multiple children, the fear of failing them educationally—but I had never had to face the fear of a pandemic, nor the fear of a government that could change society in the blink of an eye. I had never been called on to forsake gathering with the brethren. I had never lived through the threat of a disease that could overwhelm hospitals and slowly choke the breath out of its victims. I had lived most of my life in a peaceful world where life was predictable, and the challenges we faced were by and large self-inflicted, the results of our own unconventional choices. I was born long after the world wars, and even 9/11 was a distant event, occurring on the opposite side of the country. I was ill-equipped to deal with a trial of such enormous scope. I felt disoriented and scared as I tried to sort through the wildly conflicting news reports and conspiracy theories; empty grocery shelves and toilet paper shortages only compounded this fear. Everything changed so fast, and I was anxiously trying to make sense of it all.

But I had my books. I was reading *The Hiding Place*, a book about a brave Dutch family during the Nazi occupation, aloud to my children at the time, and I began to use "WWBD" as a code for how I should handle the situation. *What would Betsie do?* I asked myself, as I scrambled to find bath tissue for our large family. *What would Betsie do?* I asked, perusing empty bread shelves at the grocery stores or hauling the heavy bucket of used dishwater after cleaning up after our large household. Betsie and her sister, Corrie ten Boom, were no strangers to hardship. They were members of a devoutly Christian Dutch family, whose father was renowned in the city for his meticulous watch repair and good deeds. In the book, Corrie ten Boom recounts the slow slide into tyranny as the Nazis turned the world against their Jewish neighbors and the ten Booms tried to save as many as they could. As I read the book aloud to my family, I took mental notes and drew encouragement from their bravery in the face of adversity.

I would haul out the bucket of dishwater and think of Corrie living amid the stench of overflowing toilets in the concentration camp. I would visit several stores looking for bath tissue and think of Corrie waiting in line with her ration cards, trying to make the food stretch to feed their growing household. When our governor mandated that we all cover our faces, a move that I struggled with because of the way it separates people, I halted my complaints as I remembered the way Betsie had chastised Corrie for complaining about the fleas. Corrie could find no reason to be thankful for the menacing little parasites, but Betsie encouraged her to give thanks for everything. Toward the end of the book, they discovered that even the fleas were a small blessing, for it was the fleas that kept the guards at bay, allowing them the freedom to share the hope of Jesus with their bunkmates without fear of reprisal. The guards simply couldn't be bothered to enter and risk getting bitten by fleas. Realizing this, Corrie did thank God for the fleas, as Betsie said they should.

Betsie and Corrie were constantly oppressed, but they didn't give up hope. When the sisters face despair after a near escape, Corrie complains to her sister, wailing, "How long will it take?"[1] Betsie responds with, "Perhaps a long,

long time. Perhaps many years. But what better way could there be to spend our lives? . . . These young women. That girl back at the bunkers. Corrie, if people can be taught to hate, they can be taught to love! We must find the way, you and I, no matter how long it takes."[2]

As I read the account of their suffering, their patient and godly response to the horrors and indignities of a Nazi concentration camp, my own fears were soothed and my gaze was shifted toward heaven, toward honoring my Father in the trial. As my perspective shifted, I started to see silver linings.

It was a stern act of the will to face fear with thankfulness, though. Throughout my life, I have struggled with imagining worst-case scenarios and feeding fear. I can get sucked into the Facebook rabbit hole, reading one article after another in an attempt to make sense of a situation, but never in my life had a situation been so hard to make sense of. As I indulged in doom scrolling, reading outrageous news stories designed to stir up anxiety, I could feel the effects of a diet of fear in my body. The discomfort that I felt gave new meaning to Proverbs 17:22: "A joyful heart is good medicine, but a crushed spirit dries up the bones." It felt like I was staggering through a desert, as if fear was slowly desiccating me, and even in my sleep my teeth would clench with the weight of worry. I deeply regret that I'm not a quicker student, but this pain was a strong admonition to take action—and the ten Boom sisters led the way. I was going to be a good student and pay attention to the lessons they had for me.

Don't Feed Fear

To overcome my own fear in this season, I had to stop feeding it and start making the truth of God's Word my daily bread.

This is a practice you will need to adopt also if you want to overcome fear in your own life. This might mean you don't watch the news, or that you delete Twitter, or that you stop reading suspense novels. Our imagination is a powerful tool for good or evil, and we need to sow life by being careful of what we think about and what we meditate on. *Atomic Habits* author James Clear writes, "The more control you have over your attention, the more control you have over your future."[3] When I spent each night reading one scary headline after another, I gave the enemy a direct line to speak to me and an opportunity to seize my heart with fear of the future. When I shut down the news and created a home that was centered in the present and in God's presence, fear left.

Emily P. Freeman, an author I love, has a beautiful way of shutting down future fears. She names "the umbrella of daily grace"[4] as the place we must remain in order to live in the presence of God. We don't need to run ahead with fearful speculations of the future because today has its own troubles, and God tells us not to worry about tomorrow.

Feed Your Spirit

Corrie and Betsie ten Boom kept their minds fixed on the Word of God instead of meditating on the horrors of their situation. The ten Boom family had gathered daily to read Scripture and pray, and this created a storehouse of truth in their souls. Every morning and evening Father would read from the family Bible, while all who were in the home, whether believers or non-believers, would share in this life-giving routine. Even on the busy morning of Father's seventieth birthday celebration, they made Scripture reading the first thing. "Father stood up and took the big brass-hinged

Bible from its shelf as Toos and Hans rapped on the door and came in. Scripture reading at 8:30 each morning for all who were in the house was another of the fixed points around which life in the Beje revolved."[5]

Habits die hard, and even when they lived in the concentration camp, they kept up this daily practice. When the guards stripped them and took away their clothes, Corrie bundled their Bible in a sweater and shoved it beneath a bench during a furtive bathroom break. They used these smuggled portions of Scripture to inspire hope. They carefully pieced out the Scriptures, one page at a time, so that others could be encouraged as well, hiding the Word under their dresses and in their hearts so they could survive the unthinkable through the power of God. Corrie later said, "As for us, from morning until lights-out, whenever we were not in ranks for roll call, our Bible was the center of an ever-widening circle of help and hope. . . . The blacker the night around us grew, the brighter and truer and more beautiful burned the word of God."[6]

> Corrie and Betsie ten Boom kept their minds fixed on the Word of God instead of meditating on the horrors of their situation. The family had gathered daily to read Scripture and pray, creating a storehouse of truth in their souls.

They took comfort in the promise from Romans, "Who shall separate us from the love of Christ? Shall tribulation, or distress, or persecution, or famine, or nakedness, or danger, or sword?" (Romans 8:35). Even as they were suffering from tribulation and distress, from persecution and hunger and nakedness and danger, they recognized that nothing could separate them from the love of God. They had hidden his Word in their hearts, and no cruel Nazi could steal it from them.

As I faced my own fears for the future through the pandemic season, Psalm 37 became a lifeline for me. As I weaned myself off an overdose of news, fearing big government and big disease, verse 11, "The meek shall inherit the land and delight themselves in abundant peace," was my comfort and strength. I memorized Psalm 23 as I faced my fears, and peace flooded my heart as I recited the truth that "yea, though I walk through the valley of the shadow of death, I will fear no evil: for thou art with me" (KJV). The promises of God were a lifeline when the world looked dark and menacing.

Maybe you already faithfully read and memorize Scripture and can say a hearty amen to the power of the Word to strengthen us in hard times. For some of us, it can be a struggle to put down the addictive phone with all the gripping headlines in order to read the quiet pages of the Bible. It can be easy to overlook God's Word when we are busy just trying to survive the intense years of raising small children; as they grow and we encounter failure as parents, it can be tempting to numb out instead of pressing into the merciful promises of God. But the promises are there for you and for me. Jesus is calling us with words of hope that will be the strength we need when we are afraid. We need to hold tightly to his Word, but how do we do that when fear overwhelms us? I think these practices can help.

1. Read the Word Aloud

We start and end every day with Scripture reading. It might be just a verse as part of our morning time devotional, or it might be whole passages, but because we've made it a habit, a day now feels incomplete and broken if we don't read Scripture aloud. We take Psalm 119 to heart and make God's Word a delight, a lamp, and our daily bread.

2. Memorize the Word

We've used resources such as *Sword Fighting: A Full Year of Devotions to Strengthen a Kid's Character* by Karyn Henley to help facilitate memorizing shorter passages of Scripture and familiarize our children with the Bible. We've also started using the abbreviation method to memorize longer passages. We simply write down only the first letter of each word of a passage we are trying to memorize, and in this way, we've got a handy prompt when we forget a word. The prompt for Psalm 23:1, "The LORD is my shepherd; I shall not want" (KJV), becomes "TLIMS; ISNW." In the past, when I would try to memorize Scripture, I would start to flip the order of words, but with the letter prompt I now gain fluency and can start adding longer passages to my store of verses. I have used it to memorize John 1, Psalm 23, and several other full chapters. As long as the letters are visible, my brain can recall what word they stand for, and as I gain fluency in this way, the verses can be recalled even when I can't see the abbreviations.

3. Encourage with the Word

As you begin to build an inner storehouse of Scripture, you can begin to speak it out loud to conquer fear. When fear starts to speak to you, you can respond with, "God gave us a spirit not of fear but of power and love and self-control" from 2 Timothy 1:7. When you are tempted with the lie that you are alone and in danger, you can recall Isaiah 41:10, "Fear not, for I am with you; be not dismayed, for I am your God;

I will strengthen you, I will help you, I will uphold you with my righteous right hand." When your children are struggling with their own fears of the future, you can reassure them that God promises to always be with them, "Have I not commanded you? Be strong and courageous. Do not be frightened, and do not be dismayed, for the LORD your God is with you wherever you go" (Joshua 1:9).

4. Meditate on the Word

I've often felt unsure of what it means to "meditate on the Word," but in her book *Sacred Rhythms*, Ruth Haley Barton describes a simple and time-tested method of Scripture meditation: "Lectio Divina (translated 'divine or sacred reading') is an approach to the Scriptures that sets us up to listen for the word of God spoken to us in the present moment."[7]

This method helps us to slow down in our reading by offering steps for contemplation and connection to the Word of God. You start this practice by choosing a short passage of Scripture, no more than six to eight verses. After taking a moment to quiet your heart with God, you read the passage once or twice during *lectio*, or "to read," looking for a word or sentence that God wants you to focus on. The second part, *meditatio*, or "to reflect," is an opportunity to contemplate the word that is highlighted. You can ask yourself how it impacts your life, or how you can adapt your life to the Word of God.

The third move, *oratio*, or "to respond," is an invitation to move toward God in light of Scripture. Maybe that means you confess that fear has been coming against you and ask God to take it away, or maybe you take a moment to forgive yourself for the ways fear has caused you to be impatient with those you love. The last part of *lectio divina* is *contem-*

platio, an invitation to rest in God. We read the passage one last time, enjoying the presence of God as we draw closer to him through his Word. I created a cheat sheet of these steps and tucked it in my Bible so that instead of rushing through my personal morning Bible times, I could move closer to God and farther from fear as I meditated on his Word.

5. Sing the Word

Singing Scripture through hymns, silly songs, and choruses has been an important part of remembering God's Word and fighting fear. When we created The Good Gospel, our Peaceful Press Sunday school resource (available at thepeacefulpress. shop/products/peaceful-press-the-good-gospel), we included twenty-six Scripture songs because we know that singing is a simple way to hide Scripture in our heart, and songs can sometimes be recalled more easily in a crisis. I started singing Scripture with my children early on, and the music of The Donut Man, Steve Green, and Judy Rogers still plays in my head, helping me to quickly recall meaningful verses.

6. Live by the Word

Overcoming fear takes action and putting the truth we have learned into practice. It's not enough to acknowledge that you are afraid; overcoming takes pushing into understanding *why* you are afraid or pushing into life and doing something you are afraid of. One of the most compelling parts of *The Hiding Place* was when Corrie tried to place a Jewish baby in a safe home. The city house they lived in was a risky place to keep a baby, with its close proximity to neighbors, so they contacted a pastor who lived in a rural area, asking if he would take the baby. He allowed fear to paralyze him, refusing to house the infant and mother out of fear that he would lose his life. If he had recalled the Scriptures, he would have remembered that we are called to love our neighbor as ourselves and that we are to defend the orphan and the widow. Instead, he refused to help, receiving a stern rebuke from Corrie's father: "You say we could lose our lives for this child. I would consider that the greatest honor that could come to my family."[8]

Her father considered loving a neighbor—even a helpless, tiny Jewish neighbor—a higher calling than saving his own life. He didn't just know the Word of God in his head, he lived by it too. Most of us aren't being called on to face death as we overcome fear, but I want to have that same spirit that strengthened the ten Boom family. In our family we face our fear, and in the process build faith and endurance through small challenges.

I face my fear of children getting injured by being willing to go on adventures with them, whether it's crossing rushing creeks on late spring hikes or careening down a river in a rubber raft my daughter is guiding. I face my fear of sickness by being willing to visit orphans and the lonely. I face the fears I have for my children's futures by imagining the best outcomes instead of the worst. When we are on a hike and I start fearing them getting hurt, I take those thoughts captive and call them what they are. I remind myself that God is good and call out the lies that are trying to speak to me; I replace those lies with Scripture and imagine a good outcome instead of a morbid one. We keep doing the things that scare us, and we become braver in the process. We do it scared.

7. Sit with the Word

We spent the last school year memorizing John 1 in both English and Latin, repeating, "In the beginning was the

Word, and the Word was with God, and the Word was God" (John 1:1). Each week, our awareness grew that the Word of God isn't just a book of lessons and guidelines for living. It's alive. It's a mystery how the Word and the Living Word can be the same, but it's true. Jesus is the Living Word, and he is here to give us the power to believe that we aren't alone. We don't have to be afraid any longer.

Overcoming fear has been a long process for me. It's like peeling an onion. It comes off in layers, and I seem to have overcome one fear only to find that another begins to plague me. I have to peel down to another layer. In this process, I've found that Jesus has been the friend who sticks closer than a brother. Jesus said, "I am with you always, to the end of the age" (Matthew 28:20). Sometimes it feels like the world is ending, but when I ask Jesus to come and be with me, to show me where fear first started lying to me, he comes. He has come to show me where he was and to comfort me in those memories so they no longer haunt and traumatize my heart, keeping me trapped in a cycle of fear.

He has come to my memory of being molested as a child and shown me the angel who opened the door and frightened the molester, halting the evil that was happening. He has come to my memory of being alone and afraid during a terrifying thunderstorm as a young child—and in the memory, I see him picking me up and holding me. Jesus has come to my memories to mother me through the hardest parts of my life, to take away the fear of abandonment and injury, and to assure me that in his arms I am safe. When he says he is with you always, he means it. He is right beside us all the time, and he wants to reveal himself to you. He wants to help you feel safe. He wants to sit with you and comfort you where fear has taken hold. Fear is the opposite of faith, and perfect love casts out fear. First John 4:18 says, "There is no fear in love, but perfect love casts out fear."

A Better Work

So much of our journey as women involves self-help—trying to do the right things so we can overcome our bad habits and become more—something different and better. We try to put something on to make ourselves lovable. But Jesus wants to do something even better for us. He wants to peel off the layers that have hidden who we are and reveal our true selves. He wants to bring us back to who we were before we were afraid. He wants to set us free to be the happy and creative little girl, the one who felt like a princess, who twirled in the sun, who gave hugs freely, who felt she could conquer the world. And when we are free from fear and fully ourselves, we can lead our children into freedom as well.

> Jesus wants to bring us back to who we were before we were afraid. And when we are free from fear and fully ourselves, we can lead our children into freedom as well.

I've taken up new hobbies, splashed in countless creeks with my children, jumped on fast-moving subways in Italy, walked through the streets of Moshi, Tanzania, at dusk, camped and hiked, white-water rafted with my daughter as the guide, started a business, and spoken on huge stages, all because I've used these tools to overcome fear and walk into freedom. My children have traveled to faraway countries, earned degrees, and sung on stages, all because we have used these tools to walk into freedom. We've let our literary heroes pave the way and have stepped into our role as pioneers with them, paving a path through the wilderness of fear. We've redeemed the years that fear had stolen, and we are now living a wild and beautiful life together.

As Corrie ten Boom overcame her own fear and learned to forgive her enemies, she was able to lead others to overcome as well. When they were still suffering the cruel reality of the concentration camp, Betsie dreamed of creating a place where survivors of these horrors could begin to heal. Corrie recounts, "As we prayed, God spoke to us about the world after the war. It was extraordinary; in this place where whistles and loudspeakers took the place of decisions, God asked us what we were going to do in the years ahead. Betsie was always very clear about the answer for her and me. We were to have a house, a large one . . . to which people who had been damaged by concentration-camp life would come until they felt ready to live again in the normal world."[9]

When the war was over, this is what Corrie did. She planted gardens with people and helped bring about reconciliation, forgiveness being the natural harvest of their love. "As flowers bloomed or vegetables ripened, talk was less of the bitter past, more of tomorrow's weather."[10]

Corrie didn't just overcome fear for her own sake. Her freedom helped lead multitudes out of bitterness and fear and into joy. As we break free from fear and start listening to and abiding in the living Word, our freedom will be a standard. We will be people who empower our children to break free. We will mother with confidence because we know our Daddy in heaven has our back. We will step into the wild and beautiful life of faith.

CHAPTER THIRTEEN
Study Guide

When have you felt most afraid?

Ask Jesus what lies you believed because of that incident. Pray the "1-2-3 Skidoo" prayer from chapter 8, asking God to send away any lies that have been plaguing you.

Ask Jesus to come close to you in the memory where you first felt afraid. Ask him to comfort you in this memory.

A VERSE TO MEMORIZE

What Scriptures comfort you when you are afraid? Some possibilities are Psalm 23, Psalm 37, and Psalm 91. Memorize the verse most comforting to you.

MORE BOOKS ON

Knowing Scripture

To Read Aloud
Twenty and Ten by Claire Huchet Bishop
Psalm 23 by Richard Jesse Watson
Goliath Must Fall for Young Readers by Louie Giglio

For Mom
The Endless Steppe by Esther Hautzig
Evidence Not Seen by Darlene Deibler Rose
Becoming Myself by Stasi Eldredge

Sing to Shut Up Fear

LITERATURE COMPANION: *The Door in the Wall*

Sleep, sleep, my love, my only, Deep, deep, in the dung and the dark; Be not afraid and be not lonely!

E. B. White, *Charlotte's Web*

I t was a year. First, there was the pandemic, with terrifying news reports of hospitals overflowing with the deceased. Then, while we were still processing the horrors of a world in a pandemic, we saw the heartbreaking images of violence that spurred a cry for justice. In the midst of all of this, it was an election year, with crazy news coming from all sides and resulting confusion as we tried to parse truth from lies and make a godly choice for president. In our home state of California, all was not well; churches were closed, restaurants were closed, wildfires were burning, turning the sky a morbid shade of gray, and rolling blackouts loomed as a constant threat. I packed a go-bag for our family, shoving snacks, extra clothes, and cash into a suitcase, just in case the fires got close enough to threaten our home, while praying hard that the winds would shift and the fires burn out.

We live in a beautiful mountain area, with crystal-clear alpine lakes a short drive from our house, but during the fires, we were forced indoors to avoid the ashy skies and sharp sting of smoke in our lungs. The outside temperatures were over a hundred degrees when our electricity was shut off to prevent lines from falling and starting more fires, during a week when the wind blew hot and fierce. It felt apocalyptic—wind, smoke, heat, our indoors nearly as hot as the temperatures outside, and no escape from the horror California was facing. We drove to the beach one day to try to get out of the smoke, and it wasn't until we were standing right on the edge of the seashore with the waves sweeping over our toes that the air cleared a bit, and we could breathe freely.

We were faced with all these external pressures, while in our little family circle, the dynamic was quickly shifting, causing its own small tremors. Since I had my first baby twenty-eight years ago, I had been inundated with the joy and purpose of caring for children, gaining deep satisfaction from my role as a mother, and when COVID hit, I even had the pleasure of having all my chicks, even the adults, under my roof for a season.

But life was moving fast, and their feathers were coming in. First, my second son left for Coast Guard boot camp, donning a mask for many hours each day to manage military life in a pandemic. We had no contact with him for several months, and I prayed as I never had as I faced the fearful experience of having a child far from home and out of reach. Next, my oldest boy graduated from college and moved across the country, trading small-town life for a big city and a big corporation as he found his way in the world. Finally, my oldest daughter headed back to her home in Northern Ireland to finish a doctorate program in law. I wept as my daughter left, the accumulation of good-byes over the summer suddenly overflowing into grief.

I went from having a houseful of children to having just a few to care for, and while there had been breakthrough after breakthrough in my fight against fear, the circumstances all changed so quickly, and fear again began to plague me. I worried about the health and safety of my children scattered across the world. I worried about the well-being of the ones still at home as we adjusted to pandemic life. I worried about the election and the fires and people in the rioting cities and hungry people in developing nations.

Maybe you've experienced the same. You thought that fear and worry no longer had permission to speak to you, and yet when circumstances changed or you entered a new season, suddenly they were there again, stealing your joy, grinding your face in the dirt. But overcoming fear is a journey, not a destination, and as with all good journeys, pitfalls and roadblocks will occur. They don't have to be the end of us. We can brush ourselves off and keep moving forward.

The Door in the Wall is a story that echoes this theme. In the book, a medieval boy is far from his family while the plague ravages his village. He is suffering from the after-effects of the disease, and his legs no longer will carry him. Stranded in his bed, with the last of the servants down with the plague, he lies there helpless and afraid. His situation is dire, and while it's hard for us to relate to the terror experienced by medieval families, when war and disease could wipe out entire villages, we've all just lived through our own twenty-first-century plague and can attest to the terror that results when we're faced with a mysterious sickness.

Thankfully, our little medieval friend Robin isn't left there to die. A kindly monk comes along who hefts him onto his back as they set out on a journey to find his parents. Together, along with a minstrel, they begin the arduous journey on foot—and as they walk, they sing. The journey becomes not only a path to his parents but also a path to hope as the minstrel teaches him to find joy through the sound of the harp and his voice.

Singing has been a path to hope for me as well. When I can't quite shake off fear and I'm tempted to stay in my head cultivating fearful thoughts instead of enjoying my children and my life, singing brings me back to the present. When life is a struggle and we've forgotten all the good tools to help us be brave, singing is a reboot, shutting down the what-ifs and worst-case scenarios and filling our hearts with peace.

It's not just that we feel more peaceful when we sing. Studies attest to the fact that singing lowers levels of cortisol, the hormone that indicates stress. When we sing, we are giving our brains a break from worry, which increases our sense of well-being. According to research compiled by Jacques Launay and Eiluned Pearce, "Singing has also been shown to improve our sense of happiness and wellbeing. Research has found, for example, that people feel more positive after actively singing than they do after passively listening to music or after

> When life is a struggle, and we've forgotten the good tools to help us be brave, singing is a reboot, shutting down the what-ifs and worst-case scenarios and filling our hearts with peace.

chatting about positive life events. Improved mood probably in part comes directly from the release of positive neurochemicals such as β-endorphin, dopamine and serotonin."[1]

When we sing, fear flees and our body is flooded with life-giving endorphins, even while the immune system killer cortisol is lowered.

Our Heroes Sang

So many of our literary heroes found the strength to overcome fear through song. When Ma was living on the lonely prairie where wolves the size of ponies prowled and there was not a single neighbor for miles, she sang: "That afternoon the wind blew fiercely and it was cold. Ma called Mary and Laura into the house. She built up the fire and drew her rocker near it, and she sat rocking Baby Carrie and singing softly."[2]

For the sailors on board the *Endurance*, stranded in the icy wasteland of Antarctica, singing was a matter of survival: "In spite of the disappointing progress, they celebrated Christmas festively. . . . Afterward, there was a hearty songfest, with Hussey playing a one-stringed violin he had made himself."[3] When Wilbur was tired and worried about becoming the Christmas ham, Charlotte the spider sang him a lullaby to put his mind at ease, "Sleep, sleep, my love, my only, Deep, deep, in the dung and the dark; Be not afraid and be not lonely!"[4]

Singing is a universal language to overcome fear and anxiety, and when we sing, we join our literary heroes in pushing back the darkness and claiming that right at this moment, right in the midst of crying babies, and homework left undone, and sickness, and money woes, we can still find joy. Singing speaks to our children, reassuring them that if Mama is singing, all will be well. Singing brings our breath together;

it organizes our breathing patterns—whether as an individual or in a group—and helps us prepare for morning time moments with joy. Singing is the prayer we pray when we've got no strength to pray. Singing is the reset button on a day gone bad.

Some of you feel like you can't sing. You've been told your voice is deficient, or your tone is off. Pay no mind to that nonsense. Your kids don't care how well you sing, and your spirit, longing for peace, doesn't care either. Your voice matters, and it's of no importance whether your pitch is perfect. Your peace is precious, so just open your mouth and let the sound come out, because when we are singing, we can't be worrying. Singing shuts down fear and buys us time to start using our tools.

There have been moments when I was so upset and afraid that I couldn't remember the words to sing. The many hymns and choruses I have sung throughout my years as a mother would escape my mind, and fight-or-flight mode shut down my memory, sweeping away the mental store of music. But there was one silly little song that I could always pull out, and when my kids heard me singing, it was both an invitation to joy and an awareness of how hard I was fighting for that joy: "Ho, ho, ho, Hosanna, Ha, ha, hallelujah. He, he, he, he saved me, and I've got the joy of the Lord!"[5]

Even if I wasn't feeling it, even if fear for my children's futures, disappointment in myself as a mother, and worry about how I would manage were swirling in my head, when I sang that little song, my mood would lighten and joy would come. The laughter-inducing song was enough to help me grab on to the arsenal that I'd developed to fight fear. Singing, for just a moment even, bought me mental space so that I could reincorporate the tools.

You might need that little reset also, so you can fight for joy. So you can stir up courage and bravery and step back into the ring. The kids are watching, and our time with them is too short to squander. When we let go of fear, we step into life. We get open horizons for fun and creativity and faith.

When I had been in this fight against fear for a few years, when I had learned to take my thoughts captive, to forgive myself, to stick to good habits, and to speak life over myself, an opportunity opened for our family to go on a mission trip to Africa. The fact that I even considered the trip was a miracle. When we left our missionary adventure in Mexico, I was bone weary and had no desire to pursue missions again. I'd spent so much of those years in fear and weariness, and it was a confirmation of the healing work of the Holy Spirit that I was willing to leave our safe home and head to a new continent to share God's love.

This trip was redemptive in so many ways. All seven of our children were with us, and while my husband and I helped facilitate a marriage workshop for missionaries, our children were caring for the missionary kids and leading them through some of the very same tools. While we were helping the mamas and papas work through forgiving each other, the kids were also learning about forgiveness. When the parents were taking captive the thoughts that had been stealing life and courage from them, the children were doing the same. The hope and life that had been restored to our family as we learned how to overcome fear was now being passed on to others. It brought to mind the story I told at the beginning of this book of Joy Clarkson confidently waving her bubble wand, believing that she could put beauty back into the world just like God did. When we overcome fear and step into a life of joy and faith, our children are right behind us, stepping into their own destiny as world changers. Our faith empowers them to believe that they too can make a difference.

The stories of brave people that I read aloud to my children inspired my son to race his boss to the hospital when the man chopped his arm with a chainsaw, instead of freezing in fear. The tools we used empowered my daughter to face life in a foreign country as a student, and having overcome her disordered eating and depression, she was able to carry a fellow student through a life-threatening fight against depression.

> The battle will be fierce, and there will be highs and lows. Overcoming fear and worry isn't a one-time event. But when we don't quit, we win.

The battle will be fierce, and there will be highs and lows, but we will overcome when we stay in the fight. We will get knocked down; overcoming fear and worry isn't a one-time event. But when we don't quit, we win.

A Love Letter for the Fight

At the end of the summer, when my oldest daughter left for Northern Ireland to finish her law degree, she could see that I was once again embroiled in a fight against fear and doing my best to be brave. She had seen me overcome my fear of harm befalling my children as we walked through a granite canyon while the rain gently dripped over us and thunder and lightning boomed threateningly. She saw me overcome my worries for my sons as I sent them on their adventure with a blessing instead of scared tears. And she saw me overcome my fear of being alone as I got on a plane to head to a conference in a strange city. But as the summer fires and coronavirus restrictions wore on, she could see the wide-eyed look start to appear again. She left me a letter of encouragement in that fight, and I want to leave it with you. "Mommy, you are wonderful, powerful, and not a victim. Get up and get dressed, worship more, sing the old songs, sing the new ones, take your thoughts captive, don't be afraid. Nothing justifies fear in any of us. I love your whimsy and sense of adventure. Ask brave questions and be beautiful, be pure, be lovely, look people in the eyes, and be fearless."

This is the letter I want to leave with you as well.

> *Be brave, be fearless.*
> *Sing the old songs and the new ones.*
> *Take your thoughts captive. Don't be afraid.*
> *You are wonderful, powerful, and not a victim.*
> *Your whimsy and sense of adventure are life-giving for you and your children.*
> *Be pure, be lovely, look people in the eyes, and be fearless.*

In the very last scene of *The Door in the Wall*, when Robin finally makes it to the courts where his mother is waiting for him, he sings for her. It's a gift to her, and it's his anthem, his celebration of overcoming the weariness and fear that had dogged him on his journey.

And one day, we will sing in the courts. We will be in the presence of our Father, singing our anthem of faith. We will celebrate that we overcame by the blood of the Lamb and the word of our testimony.[6] We will celebrate that we ran the race with endurance because joy was set before us. The war will be over; eternal joy will be ours.

But for now, we sing in hope. We trust that while we can't yet see him, we have a loving Father who is watching over us and who tells us, "Do not be afraid." We celebrate his faithfulness each time we take up our books and our Bibles and say no to fear and a hearty yes to the life of faith. We celebrate his faithfulness each time we bake cookies with our kids instead of sitting paralyzed on the couch. We are a living testimony of faith, of trusting that God loves us and will care for us, in every poetry reading, and nature outing, and when we are running to the bathroom with a toddler, and when we are once again trying to make sense of a math problem with a teen. With every loving action and word, we are saying no to fear and yes to love. We are an anthem of joy as we slay fear for the children's sake.

CHAPTER FOURTEEN
Study Guide

Which tools will you start with in the fight against fear?

A VERSE TO MEMORIZE

Make a joyful noise unto the LORD, all ye lands.
Serve the LORD with gladness: come before his presence with singing.

PSALM 100:1–2 KJV

SONGS TO
Lighten Your Heart

"Ho, Ho, Ho Hosanna"
"The Joy of the Lord Is My Strength"
"We're Getting Ready" by Maverick City Music

MORE BOOKS FOR
Overcoming Fear

To Read Aloud
It Will Be Okay by Lysa TerKeurst
Good Good Father by Chris Tomlin and Pat Barrett
The Courage of Sarah Noble by Alice Dalgliesh

For Mom
The Story of the Trapp Family Singers
by Maria Augusta Trapp
*A Chance to Die: The Life and Legacy of Amy
Carmichael* by Elisabeth Elliot
Breaking the Fear Cycle by Maria Furlough

Acknowledgments

So many people contributed to the culmination of this project, and words alone can't express my gratitude. First, I'd like to thank Emily P. Freeman, Brian Dixon, and Gary Morland as well as the Hope Writers Mastermind group for their fantastic encouragement as this project was being developed.

I'd also like to thank my agent, Ingrid Beck, and my editors, Jennifer Dukes Lee and Sharon Hodge, for being such fantastic advocates and wordsmiths.

My sisters Jacqueline, Jody, LeeAnn, and Tammi, and friends Melissa and Laura lovingly read and commented on the manuscript, and I'm grateful for their feedback and friendship.

My daughter Emelie has been a friend who sticks closer than a brother, and her willingness to let her story be shared so that others might find freedom inspires courage in me. I'm so thankful for her love and input.

My parents, John and Rosalind, are amazing. Their loyalty to each other and to their children has kept us close, and their faith in God through many adversities has strengthened my own faith. I'm so glad to be their daughter.

Notes

Chapter 1: Let Literature Free Us from Fear

1. Maria Furlough, *Breaking the Fear Cycle: How to Find Peace for Your Anxious Heart* (Grand Rapids, MI: Revell, 2018), 86.

2. Elizabeth Barrett Browning, *Aurora Leigh* (New York: C. S. Francis & Co., 1857), 275.

3. Sally Clarkson, *Awaking Wonder: Opening Your Child's Heart to the Beauty of Learning* (Minneapolis, MN: Bethany House, 2020), 18.

Chapter 2: Overcome the Fear of Being Alone through Journaling

1. Anne Murray, "You Needed Me," *Let's Keep It That Way*, Capitol Records, 1978.

2. Jane Austen, *The Works of Jane Austen* (Ann Arbor Media Group, 2006), 310.

Chapter 3: Overcome the Fear of the Baby Years by Staying Present

1. Ruth Hulburt Hamilton, "Song for a Fifth Child," *Ladies' Home Journal*, October 1958, 186.

2. Celestia and Steven Tracy, *Forever and Always: The Art of Intimacy* (Eugene, OR: Wipf and Stock, 2011), 68–69.

3. Zephaniah 3:17.

4. Luke 12:7; Matthew 10:30.

5. Edward Zigler, "Formal Schooling for Four-Year-Olds? No," in *Early Schooling: The National Debate*, ed. Sharon L. Kagan and Edward F. Zigler (New Haven, CT: Yale University Press, 1987), 27–44.

6. David Elkind, *Miseducation: Preschoolers at Risk* (New York: Knopf, 1997), 4.

7. See Deuteronomy 31:6, my paraphrase.

Chapter 4: Overcome the Fear of Failure by Speaking Life

1. E. B. White, *Charlotte's Web* (New York: Harper and Brothers, 1952), 80.

2. White, *Charlotte's Web*, 114.

3. Andrew Newberg, MD, and Mark Robert Waldman, *Words Can Change Your Brain: 12 Conversation Strategies to Build Trust, Resolve Conflict, and Increase Intimacy* (New York: Avery/Penguin Random House, 2012), 34.

4. White, *Charlotte's Web*, 183.

5. Lloyd John Ogilvie, *When You Need a Miracle: Experiencing the Power of the God of the Impossible* (Eugene, OR: Harvest House, 1984), 30.

6. White, *Charlotte's Web*, 31.

Chapter 5: Overcome the Fear of My Children Being Behind through Balance

1. Dorothy Canfield Fisher, *Understood Betsy* (Littleton, CO: Sonlight Curriculum, 1996), 3.

2. Fisher, *Understood Betsy*, 3.

3. Greg McKeown, *Essentialism: The Disciplined Pursuit of Less* (New York: Crown Business, 2014), 5.

4. John Taylor Gatto, *Weapons of Mass Instruction: A Schoolteacher's Journey through the Dark World of Compulsory Schooling* (Gabriola Island, BC: New Society Publishers, 2009), 60.

5. Ainsley Arment, *The Call of the Wild and Free: Reclaiming Wonder in Your Child's Education* (San Francisco: HarperOne, 2019), 4.

6. Gatto, *Weapons of Mass Instruction*, 84.

7. Peter Gray, "Early Academic Training Produces Long-Term Harm," *Psychology Today*, May 5, 2015, https://www.psychologytoday.com/us/blog/freedom-learn/201505/early-academic-training-produces-long-term-harm.

8. Gray, "Early Academic Training."

9. Fisher, *Understood Betsy*, 92

10. As quoted in Peter Downs, *Schoolhouse Shams: Myths and Misinformation in School Reform* (Lanham, MD: Rowman & Littlefield, 2013), 34.

11. Fisher, *Understood Betsy*, 45.

12. Gatto, *Weapons of Mass Instruction*, 123.

13. William Rohwer Jr., "Prime time for education: Early childhood or adolescence?" *Harvard Education Rev* 41, no. 3 (September 1971): 316–341.

Chapter 6: Overcome the Fear of Children Leaving the Faith through Family Identity

1. Sydney Taylor, *All-of-a-Kind Family* (New York: Yearling, 1951), 78.
2. Abraham Joshua Heschel, *The Sabbath* (New York: Farrar, Straus, and Giroux, 1951), 60.
3. Taylor, *All-of-a-Kind Family*, 93.
4. Leonard Sax, *The Collapse of Parenting: How We Hurt Our Kids When We Treat Them Like Grown-Ups* (New York: Basic Books, 2016), 109.
5. Lifeway Research, "Most Teenagers Drop Out of Church When They Become Young Adults," Lifewayresearch.com, January 15, 2019, https://lifewayresearch.com/2019/01/15/most-teenagers-drop-out-of-church-as-young-adults/.

Chapter 7: Overcome the Fear of Failing Our Children by Living for a Greater Purpose

1. Ephesians 4:1.
2. E. Nesbit, *The Railway Children* (United Kingdom: Puffin Books, 1906), 15.
3. Greg McKeown, *Essentialism: The Disciplined Pursuit of Less* (New York: Crown Business, 2014), 26.
4. Charlotte Mason, *Towards a Philosophy of Education* (Carol Stream, IL: Tyndale House, 1989), 2.
5. Abraham Joshua Heschel, *The Sabbath* (New York: Farrar, Straus, and Giroux, 1951), 27.
6. McKeown, *Essentialism*, 26.
7. John Calvin's *Institutes of the Christian Religion* on Reformed .org, https://reformed.org/books/institutes/books/book1/bk1ch01.html.
8. See Philippians 1:6.
9. N. D. Wilson, *Death by Living: Life Is Meant to Be Spent* (Nashville: Thomas Nelson, 2013), 42.
10. Robert Frost, "A Servant to Servants" in *Early Poems* (New York: Penguin, 1998), 87.
11. Brennan Manning, *Ruthless Trust: The Ragamuffin's Path to God* (New York: HarperCollins, 2009), 2.
12. Julian of Norwich, *Revelations of Divine Love*, as quoted in "Silence," Alban at Duke Divinity School, December 18, 2006, https://alban .org/archive/silence.

Chapter 8: Overcome the Fear of the Future by Not Complaining

1. Scarlet Hiltibidal, *Afraid of all the Things: Tornadoes, Cancer, Adoption, and other Stuff You Need the Gospel For* (Nashville: B&H Publishing, 2019), 25.

2. Laura Ingalls Wilder, *These Happy Golden Years* (New York: Harper Trophy, 1971), 52.

3. Wilder, *Little Town on the Prairie*, 89.

4. Jennie Allen, *Get Out of Your Head: Stopping the Spiral of Toxic Thoughts* (Colorado Springs: Waterbrook, 2020), 42.

5. Dr. Travis Bradberry, "How Complaining Rewires Your Brain for Negativity," TalentSmartEQ.com, accessed November 20, 2021, http://www.talentsmart.com/articles/How-Complaining-Rewires-Your-Brain-for-Negativity-2147446676-p-1.html.

6. Allen, *Get Out of Your Head*, 38.

7. Barry and Lori Byrne, *Love After Marriage Workshop Workbook* (Love After Marriage, 2008), 50–51.

8. Aundi Kolber, *Try Softer: A Fresh Approach to Move Us Out of Anxiety, Stress, and Survival Mode—and into a Life of Connections and Joy* (Carol Stream, IL: Tyndale, 2020), 28.

9. *Merriam-Webster*, s.v. "grit," accessed January 11, 2022, https://www.merriam-webster.com/dictionary/grit.

10. Kelsie Anderson and Aubrey Francisco, "The Research Behind the TED Talk: Angela Duckworth on Grit." *Digital Promise*, March 6, 2019, digitalpromise.org/2019/03/06/research-behind-ted-talk-angela-duckworth-grit.

11. Laura Ingalls Wilder, *The Long Winter* (New York: Harper Collins, 1940), 223.

12. 1-2-3 Skidoo prayer used with permission from Nothing Hidden Ministries.

Chapter 9: Overcome the Fear of Not Having Enough through Thankfulness

1. Ralph Moody, *Little Britches: Father and I Were Ranchers* (Lincoln, NE: University of Nebraska Press, 1950), 14.

2. Ann Voskamp, *One Thousand Gifts: A Dare to Live Fully Right Where You Are* (Grand Rapids, MI: Zondervan, 2010), 151.

3. Voskamp, *One Thousand Gifts*, 118.

4. Hervey Wilbur, *The Assembly's Shorter Catechism, with the Scripture Proofs in Reference: with an Appendix on the Systematic Attention of the Young to Scriptural Knowledge* (Newburyport, MA: Wm. B. Allen & Co., 1816), 2.

5. Dane Ortlund, *Gentle and Lowly: The Heart of Christ for Sinners and Sufferers* (Wheaton, IL: Crossway Books, 2020), 160.

6. Moody, *Little Britches*, 249.

7. G. K. Chesterton, *Collected Works: Collected Poetry, Part 1*, comp. Aidan Mackey (San Francisco, CA: Ignatius, 1994), 38.

8. Moody, *Little Britches*, 260.

Chapter 10: Overcome the Fear of Not Being Able to Manage by Building Good Habits

1. Ted Tripp's book *Shepherding a Child's Heart* describes a traditional Christian parenting method with an emphasis on reaching your child's heart. Waldorf is an educational philosophy based on the work of Rudolf Steiner with an emphasis on creativity and play in the early years.

2. Frank B. Gilbreth and Ernestine Gilbreth Carey, *Cheaper by the Dozen* (New York: T.Y. Crowell Co., 1948), 2.

3. Charlotte Mason, *Home Education* (Carol Stream, IL: Tyndale House, 1989), 118.

4. George MacDonald as quoted in John Piper, *When the Darkness Will Not Lift: Doing What We Can While We Wait for God—and Joy* (Wheaton, IL: Crossway Books, 2006), 46.

5. James Clear, *Atomic Habits: An Easy & Proven Way to Build Good Habits & Break Bad Ones* (New York: Avery, 2018), 27.

6. Clear, *Atomic Habits*, 145.

7. Clear, *Atomic Habits*, 190.

8. Clear, *Atomic Habits*, 198.

9. Gilbreth and Carey, *Cheaper by the Dozen*, 232.

10. Gilbreth and Carey, *Cheaper by the Dozen*, 235.

Chapter 11: Overcome Fear by Running after Purpose

1. Dorothy Sterling, *Freedom Train: The Story of Harriet Tubman* (New York: Scholastic Biographies, 1987), 89.

2. Sterling, *Freedom Train*, 89.

3. Sterling, *Freedom Train*, 158.

4. Sally Clarkson, *Awaking Wonder: Opening Your Child's Heart to the Beauty of Learning* (Minneapolis, MN: Bethany House, 2020), 62.

5. Sterling, *Freedom Train*, 191.

Chapter 12: Overcome the Fear of Leading through Forgiveness

1. Alfred Lansing, *Endurance: Shackleton's Incredible Voyage* (New York: Carrol & Graf, 1959), 3.

2. Lansing, *Endurance*, 38.

3. Lansing, *Endurance*, 38.

4. Lansing, *Endurance*, 38.

5. Lansing, *Endurance*, 38.

6. Lansing, *Endurance*, 89.

7. DeVon Franklin as quoted in Katherine Schwarzenegger Pratt, *The Gift of Forgiveness* (London, England: Penguin Life, 2020), 104.

8. Cora Jakes Coleman as quoted in Schwarzenegger, *Forgiveness*, 183.

Chapter 13: Overcome Fear by Knowing Scripture

1. Corrie ten Boom, *The Hiding Place* (New York: Bantam Books, 1984), 175.

2. Ten Boom, *The Hiding Place*, 175.

3. James Clear (@JamesClear), Attention, Twitter, March 27, 2020, https://twitter.com/JamesClear/status/1243722137657106432.

4. Emily P. Freeman, Hope Writers Mastermind teaching from June 2020.

5. Ten Boom, *The Hiding Place*, 7.

6. Ten Boom, *The Hiding Place*, 194.

7. Ruth Haley Barton, *Sacred Rhythms: Arranging Our Lives for Spiritual Transformation* (Downers Grove, IL: IVP Books, 2006), 54.

8. Ten Boom, *The Hiding Place*, 99.

9. Ten Boom, *The Hiding Place*, 212.

10. Ten Boom, *The Hiding Place*, 237.

Chapter 14: Sing to Shut Up Fear

1. Jacques Launay and Eiluned Pearce, "Choir Singing Improves Health, Happiness—and Is the Perfect Icebreaker," *The Conversation*, the conversation.com, October 28, 2015, https://theconversation.com/choir-singing-improves-health-happiness-and-is-the-perfect-icebreaker-47619.

2. Laura Ingalls Wilder, *Little House on the Prairie* (New York: HarperCollins, 1992), 201.

3. Alfred Lansing, *Endurance: Shackleton's Incredible Voyage* (New York: Basic Books, 2014), 27.

4. E. B. White, *Charlotte's Web* (New York: Harper and Brothers, 1952), 104.

5. "Ho-ho-ho-hosanna," traditional, public domain, https://sermons4kids.com/ho-ho-ho-hosanna.

6. See Revelation 12:11.

About the Author

Jennifer Pepito is the founder of the Peaceful Press, an education resource company dedicated to helping families overcome fear and enjoy their children. Her writing has been featured in *Wild + Free*, *Charlotte Mason Poetry*, *Commonplace Quarterly*, and *Homeschool Enrichment*.

Jennifer is a Simplicity Parenting coach, certified life coach, and *Wild + Free* podcast host. She lives with her husband and children in the mountains of California and enjoys reading great books, drinking coffee, and hanging out with her family.